RESEARCHING
CHICANO COMMUNITIES

RESEARCHING CHICANO COMMUNITIES

Social-Historical, Physical,
Psychological, and Spiritual Space

IRENE ISABEL BLEA

Westport, Connecticut
London

Library of Congress Cataloging-in-Publication Data

Blea, Irene I. (Irene Isabel)
　　Researching Chicano communities : social-historical, physical,
　psychological, and spiritual space / Irene Isabel Blea.
　　　　p.　cm.
　　Includes bibliographical references and index.
　　ISBN 0–275–94974–5 (hc : alk. paper).—
　ISBN 0–275–95219–3 (pbk.)
　　　1. Mexican Americans—Southwest, New—Social conditions.
　2. Southwest, New—Social conditions.　I. Title.
　F790.M5B57　1995
　305.868′72073′072—dc20　　　　95–2224

British Library Cataloguing in Publication Data is available.

Library of Congress Catalog Card Number: 95–2224
ISBN: 0–275–94974–5
　　　0–275–95219–3 (pbk.)

First published in 1995

Praeger Publishers, 88 Post Road West, Westport, CT　06881
An imprint of Greenwood Publishing Group, Inc.

Printed in the United States of America

The paper used in this book complies with the
Permanent Paper Standard issued by the National
Information Standards Organization (Z39.48–1984).

10　9　8　7　6　5　4　3　2　1

Illustrations by Oscar R. Castillo, Photographer

To Raven,
who has moved with me
to live and thrive in five Chicano communities.

Contents

Tables

Introduction

The discipline of Chicano Studies and focused attention to researching Chicano communities is just over 25 years old. Many of those who founded it have taught it for more than one generation and have changed distinctly the nature of education. As a young woman, I was doing graduate work at the University of Colorado, Boulder. In the 1970s I was also active addressing feminist issues in the Chicano movement and working with others to develop the Department of Chicano Studies at the university. While thus involved in the northern part of the state, I often related some things said in meetings, read in textbooks, or heard during lectures to the Bessemer Chicano community in the southern part of the state, where I had done my undergraduate work. This community was predominantly Chicano. My interest in Bessemer became the focus of my Ph.D. dissertation, which was defended in 1979 in the Department of Sociology.

I have revisited Bessemer, in person and in my work, many times. Some things have changed and some things remain the same. In this book I share my visits to Bessemer, to compare and to contrast this community to the development of Chicano Studies, which has also changed very much. This text unveils this change and compares and contrasts the Bessemer experience to other Chicano communities in the Southwest. This social-historical analysis commemorates 25 years of achievement in Chicano Studies, instructs the student on the cultural elements of doing research in Chicano communities, and presents the current condition and social issues in these communities.

Chicano Studies remains a strong academic force as it graduates students and gives academic voice to as many as 22.4 million Latinos from more than 20 different countries residing in the United States. It educates on university and college campuses, at national and international conferences, and at other meetings, and it does this in Chicano communities throughout the United States. Community empowerment via the distribution of knowledge goes on despite recent national attention to violence, drugs, and racism. Chicano Studies is a discipline that links theory to practice while stressing the positive cultural attributes of a diverse population. This book is written to assist those who want to gain more insight into the nature of Latino communities, Chicano Studies, and American gender and race relations. It makes clear the relationship of teaching and doing research in Latino communities to community empowerment. To highlight this discussion, I focus upon southwestern Chicanas (females) and Chicanos (males) because all too frequently the issues of race relations are perceived as black/white relations on the East Coast.

In this text Chicanos are also referred to as Latinos because they share language and Spanish ancestry with this diverse group of people that include Puerto Ricans, Cubans, and Central and South Americans. But, more specifically the term refers to Americans of Mexican origin and is identified with a precise ideology. This ideology will be outlined from a masculine as well as a feminist perspective. Chicana feminism is incorporated because Chicano Studies and the civil rights movement, which so heavily influenced Chicano Studies, have been inappropriately characterized as male. In addition, this text will broaden the reader's understanding of southwestern mestizos: part Indian, part Spanish European.

To facilitate the discussion I introduce the concept of space and incorporate four aspects of that space: social-historical, physical, emotional/psychological, and spiritual. I review participant observation, the methodology that was most frequently used to study Chicano communities when Chicano Studies was founded. I evaluate the strengths and weaknesses of participant observation and review the role of Chicano Studies in this "how-to-do research in the Chicano community" text.

Chapter 1 lends insight to the ethnic labeling processes, how Chicanas and Chicanos choose to define themselves as *raza* (people); and why I chose to use the word "Chicano." Chapter 2 reviews traditional social science literature to place Chicano community studies and participant observation within the context of the development of community research in the field of sociology. Chapter 3 focuses upon constructing a culturally sensitive methodology and chapter 4 centers upon entering the field and gathering data. The latter chapter also notes how technology has influenced the research process and Chicano Studies, in particular.

Bessemer was one of the first studies of a Chicano community in the nation, but it took 11 years to publish its findings. In *Bessemer: A Sociological Perspective on a Chicano Barrio* (1990), I define and analyze the structure and function of Bessemer's major social institutions and bring attention to how discrimination impacts Latinos personally, socially, spiritually, and historically. The Bessemer study established that there are mental constructions rooted in historical experience that direct the lives of the people in Chicano communities today. The fluidity by which institutions function and are utilized is most evident in chapter 5 of this text.

My early study of Bessemer went beyond the traditional Chicano Studies focus on history, education, economics, and politics to include attention to spirituality and to the lives of women. The consistency of spirituality was striking, while the gender differential was and still is significant in Bessemer. Chapter 6 is highly significant because it focuses on gender roles with strong emphasis on Chicana feminism and Chicana feminist scholarship. This is done because gender, as well as sexual orientation, influences every aspect of life, including the research process that permeates how the community is conceptualized and studied. The study of the role of women and spirituality helps formulate solutions on how to empower Chicano communities, as well as the general society.

This text will discuss how a non-finding is still a finding and how, while conducting the literature review for the 1978 Bessemer study, the lack of literature focusing upon Chicanos became evident. This is no longer the case, because a rare breed of scholars, who are now between the ages of 48 and 65, took it upon themselves to study and write about their own experiences. These early Chicano scholars struggled to gain control of and direct the content of their education. They gave birth to a second, and now a third, generation of academics who find value in Chicana and Chicano Studies. How this unique group created new educational standards and how they disseminated their knowledge are discussed in chapter 8.

Chicana and Chicano scholars have contributed to society and to academia by extending challenges to existing academic and social paradigms. The text defines and discusses paradigm construction and paradigm shift in its final chapters. Chapter 9 focuses upon contemporary issues in the Chicano community and places them within a global perspective. The chapter asserts that Latinos, unlike most Americans, live in an international setting and are frequently in sympathy with third world countries. It advocates not using the term "third world" to refer to underdeveloped countries and notes that Chicanos frequently visit other countries—they exchange letters and send money, commodities, and information back and forth between relatives, friends, and their academic counterparts. In the last chapter the author discusses social science theory and contends that Chicanos can play a major role in healing the nation from the social ills of discrimination.

Family consists of nuclear, extended and compadrazco, godparents and their family. Family very often includes lifetime friends who are not blood relatives.

1   Defining Community

Scholars studying Chicano and other Latino communities must first operationally define what is being studied. I would make an argument for a grounded definition, a definition that comes from those being studied, in order to prevent bias. In this chapter, how individuals define themselves will be analyzed. This is done by defining characteristics of the population, including labels used to refer to the population itself and how those labels came to be. The community is discussed in terms of physical, social-historical, emotional/psychological, and spiritual space. It is framed within a Chicana and Chicano perspective by briefly exploring Chicano history and the relationships among members of the group and other groups.

This chapter also sets the tone for the discussions that follow by focusing on what has been written about Chicanos and Chicanas and how Chicanos have been studied. The reader should keep foremost in mind that when the ethnic label "Chicano" is used it also refers to women. When women are singled out from the general population, the terms "Chicana," "Latina," "Hispana," and "Mexicana" will be used.

My study of the Chicano community begins by exploring what it is not. It is not always a barrio. It is not always inner city. It is not always poor. It is not always ridden with crime, and it is not always overcrowded. Many people assume that reference to the Chicano community defines a homogenous population. It does not. Many people, from diverse backgrounds, make up these communities. Individuals can originate in any of the Latino countries. They may be of mixed heritage, and they may intermarry. Reference to the Chicano community encompasses how the Chicano population lives, not only in a specific area of a town or city but throughout rural areas of the nation. Implied in this diverse definition of the community is a political connotation and the fact that historically persons in the Chicano community were confined to geographical, social, and psychological space by both external and internal forces. It is important to remember that this space also has spiritual dimensions.

By entering into a discussion of the factors comprising the Chicano community, as a physical, social-historical, and spiritual setting, a clearer definition of the Chicano community emerges. It is futile to attempt to sharply categorize these aspects of the community for they frequently overlap. For example, the spiritual element of Aztlan crosses over into its social-historical aspect because Aztlan is not only a physical region but is also a state of mind, a spiritual belief. Aztlan is not outlined on any map of this hemisphere. It is generally not studied in geography or history classes required in high school. Aztlan is the geographic area that the Aztecs said they originated from after they arrived in the central valley of Mexico in 1300 B.C.

The Chicano search for identity in the 1960s reintegrated Mexican history, spirituality, and social reality into the self-conceptualizations of Chicano communities. During this period being of Mexican origin became a part of the psyches of some members of the Chicano community. Because not everyone was involved in the Chicano movement of the 1960s, everyone does not recognize herself/himself as Chicanos or as a member of Aztlan. In fact, some community members define themselves as descendants of the Spanish conquistadors who colonized the Aztecs and Mexico. These members of the community prefer the terms "Spanish" or "Hispanic" when they self-identify. Mexican immigrants favor the terms "Mexicano" or "Mexican American," depending on when they immigrated into the country, while still others prefer "Latino." The terms "Hispano" and/or "Hispanic" are used, usually by government officials, to refer to Latinos in the nation. None of the terms, however, distinguish between the differences in race and ethnicity among this diverse population. Race has to do with genetic attributes; ethnicity has to do with cultural attributes.

Generally, the term "Chicano" refers to approximately 61 percent of the Latino population. This population is highly concentrated in the U.S. Southwest, but can also be found in other parts of the nation (U.S. Bureau of the Census, 1993.) Some southwestern Mexican Americans are the descendants of the earliest European settlers in the United States, and many are the population absorbed into the country as the result of the U.S. war with Mexico and the Treaty of Guadalupe Hidalgo signed in 1848. They also include those who immigrated following the Mexican Revolution in 1910, the Bracero Program (1942–1947), and as a result of the more recent push-pull economic and political relationship between the United States and Latin America. It is important to note that new immigrants inherited the conquered status of the Mexican Americans, resulting from the U.S. war with Mexico, and that they are treated as Chicanos by the dominant society.

SOCIAL-HISTORICAL SETTING

Communities do not exist in social or historical isolation. Not only are they defined by state and federal governments, they are prescribed by their own history prior to governmental definitions: what their ancestors did to one another, how they feel about what happened, and how they relate the past to the next generation. People inherit communities because they are born, or move, into them. Thus, they inherit what has gone on before them. Some individuals grow up to live the life that is outlined for them, wishing it were different. Others strive to change it.

As referenced above, the most recent major social change for Chicanos occurred in the 1960s with the Chicano civil rights movement. During this time communities began to host meetings where physical and social living conditions were discussed. These gatherings produced social action and addressed specific issues with education, poverty, politics, and housing moving to the forefront. Many individuals discovered their leadership qualities for the first time. From this local arena, they gained national and even international recognition.

A review of that era reveals a highly male-dominated depiction of the social movement. While women were very much at the forefront, their actions were not documented and certainly did not emerge in the media spotlight. Instead, the personalities and concentrated efforts of Cesar Chavez, Corky Gonzales, Reyes Tejerina, and Jose Angel Gutierrez got national attention. Because they were genuinely charismatic, these men well deserve attention, but the male-dominant Anglo media had much to do with creating a male-dominant image of the movement. Women were at the heart of the Chicano movement via their participation as students, farm workers, and community organizers. They were present at every level. In the true communal spirit of the culture, the work of Helen Chavez and Dolores Huerta, Jerri Gonzales and Nita Gonzales, and Luz Gutierrez contributed heavily to the movement.

Prior to the movement, Chicanos wished some aspects of life in their communities were different. They knew that they had lived, with racism, in relative peace, until the Anglos arrived in the Southwest. This is not to ignore the fact that the Spanish and their decedents imposed restrictions upon indigenous people in order to gain physical and political space on the continent, especially in the area they renamed Nueva Espana. The Spanish migrated north into what is now known as the U.S. Southwest. In New Mexico, for example, they were chased out of the region in 1680 for imposing Spanish cultural ways upon the natives of the pueblos. The Spanish did not come back until 1692, when they agreed to live in relative peace. After their return and settlement, the Spanish-speaking communities learned to respect, interact with, or ignore their differences with the native people. They thrived, building elaborate trading routes, communities with churches and stores, and a communication system.

There was great distance between the central valley of Mexico and what we now recognize as the U.S. Southwest. The region was isolated, consisting of priest-centered mission systems, military and government land holdings, plus several ranchos. The vast region barely felt the effects of the turmoil of 1821, when the Spanish colonists living well to the south, in Mexico, liberated themselves from Spain and later fought to defend Mexico from French rule.

The state of California experienced conditions that were specific to the coastal region, and certain settlement patterns are discernable. In 1542, Spanish seamen first landed on the coast. Their ships were loaded with cargo from India and China, and they were sailing to Mexico. Later expeditions were sent into the region by the viceroy of Nueva Espana. The bays they first encountered along the coast were named San Diego, Santa Barbara, and Monterey. Spanish ships did not return until a century and a half later, when Spain was informed that Russian ships were landing on the northern coast while hunting for otters and seals. At this time expeditions brought Catholic clergy and the mission system was established. The Spanish king founded a total of 21 missions along the entire coast of California.

Some differences in the settlement patterns of Chicano communities across the Southwest can be seen. Arizona, for example, had a less intense mission structure, while Colorado had none. Culturally speaking, southern Colorado is much like New Mexico, but New Mexico has a large Navajo and Zuni population. The fact that the Spanish had strongholds in what is now Florida and that they controlled the Mississippi River trade also influenced settlement patterns.

Prior to the coming of the Spanish, indigenous people had already explored and settled many regions. They had contact with other tribes and were knowledgeable about the land, the flora, and the fauna. In some regions there was vicious conflict between Indians and Spanish. In others that conflict was less intense and there was cultural exchange. One thing is clear, however; when the Anglos came, conflict with them characterized most, if not all, Spanish settlements. The arrival of pale-complected individuals brought a different language, a different way of living, and a different religion to the region. Later, many more Anglos came to live in the Spanish-speaking, Mexican communities.

Estates, churches, and forts of that time have been preserved or reconstructed, and it is known that there was a strict division of female and male labor. What is not as widely known, however, is that some of the large Spanish, and later Mexican, land grants were given directly to women. Women, like Dona Maria del Carmen Calvillo, managed ranches they had inherited from their husband or fathers (Adelante Mujeres, 1992). How women and/or groups of women coped with the racial conflict is not well documented. It is known, however, that arranged marriages were a norm in both cultures and that intermarriage was a vehicle by which rich Mexican fathers benefited from the wealth of the Anglos. Only Mexican citizens could buy land, but Anglo males could become citizens by marrying Mexican women. Mexican fathers very frequently arranged the intermarriages in order to increase, or to at least, sustain their land grant holdings.

In what is now called Texas, Anglo refusal to live according to Mexican law and the specific conditions under which Texans were allowed to live in Mexico's northern territory caused conflict. War followed. Much attention has been given to the battle of the Alamo, a small mission in a row of missions near San Antonio. Texas eventually became an independent entity and quickly joined the Anglo-dominated United States.

Since the Anglo invasion of Mexico and the signing of the Treaty of Guadalupe Hidalgo in 1848, Chicanos and Indians have resisted the influence of Anglo colonizers on the physical, psychological, and spiritual levels. It was not until after World War II that Chicano consciousness solidified in some southwestern regions and Chicanos began concentrated efforts to change their quality of life in order to define themselves and to provide for a more secure future. In the 1960s, group consciousness was at its highest. The Chicano civil rights movement put labels on how Chicanos had been treated in the United States. They called it discrimination, racism. Naming the process motivated action and better self and community definition. "Action" became the cry of the revolution, which manifested in a reform movement.

COMMUNITY LABELS AND CHARACTERISTICS

How people choose to identify themselves is important because labeling is imposing a definition. One either lives up to or down to a standard when a label is used because the label denotes value. Some things are known about how labels emerge and how they work to define groups, but not much is known about how groups come to define themselves. Nevertheless, labeling is a process that defines "in groups" and "out groups," the normal and the abnormal, the legitimate and the deviant. Labeling is subjective. It not only reflects group values, but it also gives a framework for understanding. There are, however, dangers attached to labeling. One of them is stereotyping, making generalizations about a group with insufficient knowledge. The danger lies in the fact that there is usually a very small bit of truth that gets amplified and extended as reality.

In the case of the label "Chicanos," there is some controversy. The term is not rooted in the Chicano movement but its use is. Traditionally it has had connotations of lower class and of even some deviancy, but today it is a term with political meaning chosen during the movement to self-identify. The term was chosen as resistance to the negative connotations of the word and hopes to turn it into something positive, something to be proud of.

I have chosen to use the term "Chicano" because of its ideological connotation, its ability to render an understanding that Chicanos have a great deal of social consciousness about the quality of life for U.S. Latinos. Basically, this ideology assumes that the user understands Chicano history, U.S. race relations, and the consequence of being a person of color in the stratified society of her/his country. It is a term that denotes that the user is not only aware of the community's deprived social circumstance, but that she/he lives a lifestyle that addresses discrimination against members of this very large group. In short, being Chicana or Chicano is a state of consciousness.

The psychological aspects of labeling have to do with ascertaining who are the individuals being defined and who is doing the defining. Usually individuals live up to or down to a standard depending upon who is labeling them. Those in the most powerful positions usually do the labeling. Thus, when Chicanos chose to label themselves they took control of themselves.

Labeling does not only lead to stereotyping; it can lead to associating groups of people with physical space. For African Americans the space is the ghetto, but for Chicanos the space is generally the barrio. Closely aligned with this is the deteriorated appearance of the physical space. As has been discussed, Latinos and Chicanos do not always live in predominantly Chicano communities. However, these communities are easily identified for they are characteristically isolated or distanced from the Anglo communities by freeways, railroad tracks, industrial corridors, airports, or dump sites. These communities have names—the West Side, the East Side, El Segundo; and they possess other symbols and physical boundaries—bridges, streets, ditches, rivers, and factories—which mark the beginning and ending of the physical space.

For many, the barrio implies poverty, gangs, bad smells, crowded housing, deteriorated business sections, and many people of color living in an area frequently distant from the larger central city. A barrio, however, needs to be more broadly defined as a neighborhood in which at least two languages are spoken (Spanish and English), where traditional and nontraditional food is eaten, where there is music, dancing and laughing, and where marriages, deaths, and births take place. This is a place where people work, experience stress and trauma, and entertain themselves. This is where they celebrate and think great ideas. A barrio is more than segregation. It is about integration, where intermarriage, and inter- and intra-group relationships are common and where emotional attachment is abundant. Many people love their neighborhoods. They rarely stop identifying with it because chances are they grew up in it. It does not matter whether people were born in east, west, or south central Los Angeles in California; Barellas in Albuquerque, New Mexico; Bessemer in Pueblo, Colorado; the north side or Five Points in Denver, Colorado; or the west side of San Antonio, Texas; they identify with this origination long after they have left the region because it has contributed to their self-definition.

This is not to imply that everything is wonderful in the Chicano community. It is not. Like other neighborhoods, it sometimes is characterized by violence, drug and alcohol abuse. Its characteristic boundaries go beyond what is presented by the media, however. If students believed all that was presented on television alone, they would think that Chicano communities are riddled by violence, prostitution, and other sort of crimes. For some communities this is true, but this is not true of all communities. The student must guard against such images, lest it bias her/him and not allow the sustaining elements to come forth.

The community is not only a physical and social space, it is also a psychological space where people have been conditioned, where they learn to love and discover the meaning of family, neighbors. It is a creative place, but it has emotional boundaries that exist in the mind. The segregation messages are strong. They can create a mentality that does not allow individuals to go beyond the community's borders where they will face racism, sexism, and class discrimination. The sad reality is that too many do not recognize that segregated communities are a form of discrimination.

Some Latino communities are self-sufficient. Residents almost never interact with Anglos. They do not even need to know how to speak English. Other communities are more interdependent. People leave them everyday to work, to go to the doctor, to the community college, or to the university. Yet, some of them are middle-income communities and others, like Bessemer, in Pueblo, Colorado, are working-class neighborhoods. I studied Bessemer between 1978 and 1979. I have followed up my study over the course of 15 years and have discovered that many of the social processes of discrimination are shared with other neighborhoods in other cities and other states. These similarities will be documented in this book.

SOCIAL DEMOGRAPHICS

Not all Chicanos live in the Southwest. The exact number of Chicanos is not known because Latinos are identified differently by various agencies. The United States Census (1993) believes there are between 15 and 24 million Latinos in the country; but even this number is ambiguous because of the migrant population, and because of the large number of undocumented individuals from other countries who are in the United States without immigration papers. This is against the law, and if they are Latino, they are referred to as illegal aliens.

In 1990, the fastest growing segment of the nation's population was Latino (U.S. Bureau of the Census, 1993). They constituted almost 9 percent of the nation's nearly 250 million people. Between 1980 and 1990 the Latino population grew over seven times as rapidly as that of the rest of the nation. The Mexican population is the largest Latino population. It nearly doubled in size between 1970 and 1980, then nearly doubled again by 1990 (U.S. Census, 1993). In 1990, nearly nine of every ten Latinos lived in ten states, but they were concentrated in California, Texas, New York, and Florida. There are also large numbers of Chicanos scattered in the Midwest, mainly in Illinois (see Table 1.1).

Table 1.1
Percentage of Latino Population by State

California	34.4	New Jersey	3.3
Texas	19.4	Arizona	3.1
New York	9.0	New Mexico	2.6
Florida	7.0	Colorado	1.9
Illinois	4.0	Massachusetts	1.3

Source: U.S. Department of Commerce, Bureau of the Census. "We the American Hispanics," November 1993, pp. 2–3.

DEFINING THE DEMOGRAPHICS OF DISCRIMINATION

Most of the scholarly attention to discrimination and the Mexican American has been structural in nature. It has focused on how social institutions discriminate against Chicanos to keep the population in an oppressed state. Chicanos frequently talk about how they are kept in their place, how their place is a low space on the social ladder. The intricacies of social, psychological, and physical space work together to keep Anglos and Chicanos apart by not allowing them authentic interaction. The primary focus here should be upon displaced racial tension. This racial tension is not appropriately focused, but, instead, is based upon an inadequate assessment of who does what to whom, why, and how. There is a social-historical component to this reality. Discrimination is experienced through social practices that involve behaviors and actions that manifest over time. On behalf of the victim there is resistance and creativity, and they contribute to sustaining the relationship.

Consider the young Bessemer man who met his wife in a working-class barrio nightclub. Every winter weekend he met her at the club, danced with her, and even gave her a ride home. He waited until it was warm enough to invite her out on a date. When he did take her out, it was to a drive-in movie. I asked him why he had not taken her to dinner at a nice restaurant, bowling, or to an indoor movie during the winter. He said he took her to the drive-in because he wanted to be alone with her but also because he was uncomfortable in "gringo places." He related that he did not take her to dinner at a nice restaurant because he did not like the way Anglos looked at him, and that he really did not want to look at them. This behavior was based upon negative past experiences with Anglos in schools, at work, and in other nightclubs. On one of these occasions the young man had had to fight because an Anglo called him a "dirty Mexican." In analyzing the situation, I concluded that the drive-in offered him a sense of autonomy. It was consistent with his working-class identification. This situation made him less conspicuous, more comfortable. Thus, this young man had developed a social, psychological, and physical space that limited interaction with Anglos to times when he was forced to—for example, when he had to purchase something.

Anglos also maintain their own social, psychological, and physical space. However, their range of movement (social, psychological, and physical) is greater. The fact that the young man described above interacts on an exchange basis and that he does not control very many resources places him in an additional subordinate position.

There are several coping mechanisms the Bessemer study revealed almost 30 years ago that are still true today. Some Chicanos work with Anglos, or with "the system," to modify conflicts and discomforts. Some work within it, while some criticize and attack the system from the "outside." Yet, other members are conservative and defend the system. One thing is certain. Most Chicanos were/are not passively accepting what they have judged as injustice. Many are at an extreme disadvantage because they lack resources. Nevertheless, they continue to create ways of "dealing," and they resist.

The various models that Chicanos have developed to respond to concrete negative predicaments is still in need of more research. Rolando Juarez (1976) defines some of them as interpreting and situating within a conceptual scheme: people do what they must to survive. They very cautiously select moments and issues over which they will take a stand, and they select when they will retreat. This caution fashions the Chicano way of life and I maintain that it is much more complex than what Juarez describes. As the example of the young man who did not like to leave the Bessemer barrio illustrates, contemporary Chicanos carefully choose how, where, and when they relate with Anglos. This coping technique calls for judgment, the use of will power. For example, it is the law that young people attend public school. The mere fact that there is a law implies that there is an aura of mistrust. Chicanos, as well as other minorities, question laws because prior experience with Anglos has been to their disadvantage, especially where laws or policies enter into the picture. This socially imposed monitoring has been culturally destructive, has kept Chicanos from economic competition, has limited the discovery of their talents, and has fixated the Chicano in a depressed social position.

According to the U.S. Census, most U.S. Latinos live in family households (1993). About 70 percent of the households are maintained by married couples, and 22 percent are headed by a female with no husband—these families were concentrated among Puerto Ricans and Dominicans. It must be remembered, however, that these figures represent only those individuals who reported being members of female-headed families; therefore, it is estimated that the female-headed household figure is considerably higher. The U.S. Census reported Hispanic families headed by married couples to be 69.9 percent, 73.0 percent of the Mexican families were headed by married couples, and 76.3 of the Spanish families were headed by married couples. However, the Spanish category is misleading. It only represents those persons whose country of origin is Spain. This statistic must be examined more carefully because many Chicanos/Latinos do not want to identify themselves as Mexican or Mexican American and report their ethnicity as Spanish or Hispanic.

DEFINING THE NORM

Sometimes statistics are used to illustrate how Chicanos/Latinos differ from the rest of the U.S. population. A hypothetical norm (normative behavior) is established. Chicano differences have been interpreted as social deviance, deviation from the norm. This has influenced the research process. As an undergraduate student in the late 1960s, I wanted to do a term paper on the poverty of Mexican Americans. The professor objected to the topic because of its "lack of contribution" to the field of sociology and because of the population's lack of contribution to U.S. society. I persisted and was finally allowed to write the paper under an area of specialization in sociology known as Social Problems. Chicanos are not a social problem. They have problems with the dominant society, and they are constantly on guard to ensure that scholars do not engage in blaming the victim.

The truth is that non-Chicano social scientists have labeled "deviant" anything they do not understand. In addition, the way Chicanos relate to and value one another in the community sometimes renders the culture tolerant of some apparent destructive behavior on behalf of others. This value structure is not understood by Anglos. Local "winos" in Bessemer were examples of deviants living, and being tolerated, in the Chicano community. Although slightly ostracized, they were not treated badly. There seemed to be a sense of understanding that they were not responsible for their condition. Today, this same tolerance is often displayed toward gang members and drug addicts. The intensity of gang- and drug-related self-destruction has risen since the late 1970s, and some Chicano communities are taking action against these forces because it now hurts the entire community. Chicanos prefer to live in a part of town where these elements are minimized, with better quality housing and security; but many want, just like Bessemer Chicanos wanted during my study, to live with other Chicanos. This is not to minimize the fact that there is overwhelming outside social pressure to keep Chicanos in the barrio, it is to point out that some Chicanos live there out of choice in order to maintain social and physical space apart from Anglos.

A demographic profile of U.S. Latinos demonstrates that some are experiencing higher incomes; nevertheless, they do not earn as much money as Anglos (see Table 1.2). In 1990, 28 percent of Hispano males who were 16 years of age and over worked as operators, fabricators, and laborers. Only 19 percent of non-Hispano males held similar positions. During the same time period, roughly 39

Table 1.2
Occupation by Gender and Ethnicity, Age 16 and Over

	Hisp.F. (%)	Hisp.M. (%)	Non.Hisp.F. (%)	Non.Hisp.M. (%)
Farming, forestry, fishing	1.6	7.3	0.8	3.6
Operators, fabricators, laborers	15.2	28.1	7.2	19.2
Services	23.5	16.1	17.0	10.2
Technical, sales, administrative support	39.1	16.7	44.8	21.5
Managerial, professional	17.0	12.1	28.2	27.4

Source: U.S. Department of Commerce, Bureau of the Census. "We the American Hispanics," November 1993, p. 8.

percent of the workers concentrated in technical, sales, and administrative support positions were Hispano females. (Anglo females represented almost 45 percent of this population.) Only about 12 percent of Hispano males held managerial and professional positions compared to about 27 percent of non-Hispano males. Hispano females were represented at a higher rate than their male counterparts in that they represented 17 percent of managerial and professional positions. Also, 17 percent of non-Hispano females and 24 percent of Hispano females were in service occupations.

The median Hispano family income was $25,064, lower than the median family income of $35,225 for all U.S. households. Hispano female-headed households had lower median incomes ($12,406) than all female households with no husband present.

As has been mentioned, most Latinos, including many of those with middle and higher incomes, prefer to live in Chicano/Latino neighborhoods because of the communal feelings they render. But some have moved out to live in Anglo communities.

In general, Anglos tend to be more individualistic, have smaller families, and be Protestant, profit oriented, and upwardly mobile. While some Chicanos have adopted Anglo values, Chicanos more frequently tend to value larger families. They are strongly influenced by Catholicism, respect and value other community members, and tend to share their material goods. Americanization, crowding, and other urban factors are now threatening their respect for others and their sharing of material goods; but it is not unusual to find households with solid incomes living in lower socio-economic communities because of the cultural bond and spiritual elements found there.

In these communities there are cultural symbols, sights, sounds, and smells that are not found in other communities. The most prominent of these signs are the use of the Spanish language, a shared community history, the balancing of two very strong—Indian and Spanish—cultures, and a distinct sense of spirituality. The spiritual element of the Chicano community is not limited to that found in traditional European Western thinking. It is present in an indigenous form and can be witnessed in storytelling, theater, dance, cooking techniques, nonelectoral politics, religion, and health. While some Chicanos can name their Indian heritage, most cannot because of racism and sexism (this lack of knowledge will be clarified in upcoming chapters). Nevertheless, indigenous elements are present and they permeate the soul, the core of what constitutes identity— how people relate to the earth, the heavens, to one another. This is more than just political ideology, it is the belief in something larger than what is experienced on earth and explained by science or religion. It is a belief in a supreme being, or beings, who permeates the social consciousness to influence creativity, hope, charity, and life pursuits.

Within a Catholic tradition, spiritual components are evident in La Virgin de Guadalupe, Jesus Christ, the saints, and the holy family. They are found in the names of towns and cities, streets and rivers. Even if Chicanos are not Catholic, they feel the impact of the indigenous, the church and Christianity. It forms part of Chicano reality and is often linked with the founding of the community. It plays a role during major rites of passage, in birth, baptism, *quincenieras*, marriage, and death; and it is also seen in the art of muralists, studio painters, poets, novelists, low riders, and even in tattoos and t-shirts.

POLITICAL USE OF ACADEMIA

The above discussion should be kept in mind when conducting, analyzing, and rendering the findings of Chicano community research. Research is conducted following certain principles that will be reviewed in chapter 3. Chicano scholars found reactions to the inherent racism and sexism in these principles. Chicanas, for example, have been tainted by the biased perceptions of Anglo men and the few women who have written using white, Anglo, male-dominated paradigms and values to judge them. These conscious and/or unconscious values have made the Chicana appear passive and unimportant. Those doing biased research have overlooked the sustaining social, cultural, and spiritual components inherent to a Chicana way of life. The resulting biased paradigms have misguided U.S. social scientists and have denied them an international leadership role by imposing a much too narrow scope on their own cultural makeup.

The social sciences now go beyond creating theories and paradigms that explain what happens to people in a society. Social science research has been used to legitimize special interest opinion, to institutionalize racism and sexism, to bias public policy, to create formulas for funding social service programs, and sometimes to teach lies in history classes. In the 1960s, the social sciences were used by the U.S. government to gain an understanding of the civil discontent that characterized the nation. Chicanos have entered the dialogue outlining this discontent. Their dialogue is one of resistance to the political use of science, and they have used the social sciences to protect themselves, to counter the wrongs that have been done to their communities.

The aura of mistrust in this resistance dialogue is rooted in the fact that Chicano communities have not felt safe, even with Anglo women. Some Anglo women have adopted the above-mentioned Anglo male perspectives and behaviors. Like Anglo men, these Anglo women have adopted paradigms that are culturally biased. They have internalized these paradigms and have entered classrooms (traditionally one of the few employment opportunities for white women) across the nation intentionally or unintentionally beating the Chicano psyche.

Chicanas have had to function with a multiplicity of oppressions at several levels; and because of this, they have learned alternative ways of thinking, creating, and organizing. If taken seriously, their experiences can be used to produce new paradigms that can create a more just society. The problem, however, has been that the dominant society believes that Chicanas have nothing to teach.

Given the conditions under which Chicanas and Chicanos have had to live, the civil rights movement was bound to happen. Chicana/Chicano Studies and its analysis were certain to develop. The social situation for Chicanos was intolerable, especially for Chicanas. Sylvia Lizarraga (1988) maintains that there is a complex interconnection between women's economic exploitation and their patriarchal and racial oppression. She explains the fundamental differences between the feminism of "third world" women and that of middle-class white women in the United States. A major difference is that the struggle for emancipation by women in underdeveloped countries has been defined historically not only as one against patriarchal ideology, but also as a simultaneous, ongoing struggle against economic exploitation and political oppression. She notes that even though the theoretical formulations posited by social feminists in the United States provide the foundations for the analysis of capitalist patriarchy, these have not yet provided for a complete analysis of a combined oppression, based on class, race, and gender. This oppression is experienced by U.S. women of color as a kind of "third world" exploitation in their own country.

When a society is thus characterized, when this situation becomes intolerable, it sets up conditions either for social reform or revolution (Blea, 1988). Chicanos have explored revolution as an alternative. A few feel this is the only alternative, but most demand social reform. They want to participate in the on-going social structure, not destroy it and replace it with a new structure—which is the goal of revolution. In the social sciences they seek more revised and totally new paradigms. This helps to explain why Chicano scholars frequently are in conflict with other academics on their own campuses. It is a battle of ideas.

A major factor contributing to the slow, or lack of, movement in the social and academic paradigms is the use of power. People need power and control over their own lives. This is especially true in a competitive culture like that of the dominant American citizen. Resistance becomes a real social force when the power and ideology (the way of thinking and doing things) of the dominant group is threatened by the minority group. Struggles for power are evident in the legal cases that women and men of color have had to file in order to gain equal access to hiring on college and university campuses, promotion, and tenure. Despite this, the work of Chicanas and Chicanos is gaining national and even international importance. Chicanas, for example, have been part of political and academic dialogues in Mexico, Central and South America, Europe, and more recently in Israel. In cultural and academic exchanges, Chicanas engage in discussions on feminism and discrimination. Mexicana feminists and Chicana feminists are in constant contact. There is also dialogue with international and U.S. Anglo women in the area of business and national and international philanthropic organizations. Chicanas have had problems with Anglo women who want to dominate these exchanges, but they have created their own space. The space they have occupied is important, and it is changing as more and more Chicanas develop a feminist consciousness.

REFERENCES

Blea, Irene I. 1988. *Bessemer: A Sociological Perspective of a Chicano Barrio*. New York: AMS Press.

Jaquez, Rolando. 1976. "What the Tape Recorder Has Created: A Broadly Based Exploration into Contemporary Oral History Practice." *Aztlan: International Journal of Chicano Studies* (Spring).

Lizarraga, Sylvia. 1988. "Hacia Una Teoria Para La Liberacion de la Mujer." In Juana R. Garcia, Julia Curry Rodriguez, and Clara Lomas, eds., *Ties of Challenge: Chicanos and Chicanas in American Society*. Houston: University of Houston Press, Mexican-American Studies Program, Monograph Series No. 6.

National Women's History Project. 1922. "Adelante Mujeres." Video. Washington, D.C.

U.S. Department of Commerce, Bureau of the Census. 1993. "We the American Hispanos," November, pp. 2–3, 8.

2 Reviewing the Literature

This chapter introduces the student to two important steps in conducting research in or on Chicano communities: selecting a research topic and the review of the literature. The chapter traces the general principles of conducting research on communities: from class analysis to the analysis of race, ethnicity, and gender. In a true interdisciplinary manner, Chicano Studies scholars drew from these academic trends to propose areas of concentration within Chicano Studies both within and outside of the established disciplines of history, education, political science, sociology, anthropology, and psychology. From there, explorations of Chicano involvement in health, law, and business followed, eventually leading to student enrollment in the natural sciences, engineering, and technology. In this chapter the student is encouraged to select a research topic from any of the above fields and to begin by conducting a review of the literature. A sample review of the literature follows.

EARLY COMMUNITY STUDIES

A review of the literature in the late 1970s revealed a lack of focus upon Chicano communities. In light of this, and in preparation for my Bessemer study, I was forced to review other areas of race and ethnicity. I discovered that there was some history of conducting research in racial and ethnic communities but there was no definition or description of what characterized a Chicano community that was not fundamentally biased. These descriptions had evolved over a period of the last 30 years. In the late 1970s there were older sociological studies that documented how contemporary life was thought to be lived, but none concentrated on the daily, routine activities of Chicanos in their own community. Today some community studies have been produced that focus upon specific el-

Students and community members at a memorial service for Chicano journalist Ruben Salazar. He was killed during the Chicano moratorium, a mass demonstration against the Vietnam War, that lead to riots, 1979.

ements of the community: *curanderismo* (holistic health), car clubs (low riders), gangs, and drugs. The academic work also documents immigration, gender roles, sexual orientation, and the nature of work—not only in written form but also as videos, films, poetry, painting, and theater.

The number of published works depicting aspects of, and even entire, Chicano communities has increased dramatically since the late 1970s, so that today it is a task to track and read all the articles and books published in one year on the subject. Entire computer programs now exist to assist the researcher in locating the latest publications. Although the number of Chicano professors in this field of research is still very low, when compared to the number of Anglos, they do exist; and for the most part, they are willing to discuss with the student and the community their research topics, research methodology, and data analysis. They are also willing to discuss the editing process, the process of submission for publication and the distribution of the information gathered by research projects. This text hopes to further this latter objective in its later chapters.

While evaluating contemporary human conditions in American society, Robert Nisbet (1962) maintained that modern society had gotten so complicated and impersonal that it had caused alienation among its members. This was not true for Mexican Americans living in Bessemer in the early 1960s when I lived near the area; and it was not true in 1978–1979 when I returned to the area. By 1994, however, more and more Chicanos were beginning to feel fragmented and even disenfranchised from their own community. Because of its largeness, Nisbet maintained, society no longer met human needs and had produced in its members an endless search for community, or a feeling of belonging. In an attempt to counteract these inadequacies, Nisbet suggested the construction of small cohesive communities. As mentioned earlier, the Chicano communities of 1962 embodied the life Nisbet longed for. They were generally small communities within large communities, but some large ones, with majority Chicano populations, also existed, and they seemed to be doing a good job of nurturing their members. Essential to Nisbet's definition of community was the manageable size of the population and a feeling of togetherness. This feeling of togetherness existed in the Chicano communities of most urban areas, and it also existed in the isolated rural villages and mid-size farm communities where Chicanos lived along with Anglos.

Most research on Chicanos has been conducted in urban areas. The media has spurred the researcher of the Chicano community within large urban areas to ask if the Chicano sense of community is being threatened by the growing violence of gang warfare and alcohol and drug addiction. I would answer by saying that it is threatening the sense of community but it is also changing the character of the community. The community is no longer a safe place, especially for women, seniors, and children, in some urban areas. The social organization from which emerges feelings of belonging, through a network of kin, friends, and acquaintances who share a common experience, is getting smaller and smaller and that which remains is constantly at risk. This alienation is what caused Anglos in the 1960s to feel disenfranchised from communities in the larger cities. Nisbet's definition of the deterioration of a sense of community still holds. Chicano gang members in the large urban areas include themselves in the community, in the larger sense, but they also view themselves as sole representatives of that community. Their notion of community does not include persons outside of their "turf." Thus, they shrink the size of their community conceptually and behaviorally. They label, name the turf, and others accept this reference and contribute to making the gang members' community smaller by not taking action to keep its definition broad. Most Chicanos define their community in ways different from gang members. The community includes where raza (their people) live. In this area people rest, make their homes, earn incomes, shop, and rear children. They recognize that gang members live within their larger communities, and many struggle to get these negative forces out of their communities.

THREE TYPES OF COMMUNITY STUDIES

Since the 1920s the three most frequent types of community studies have been ethnographic studies, social stratification studies, and studies concentrating on race relations (Poplin, 1972). These three types of studies can be found in Chicano Studies. Studies concentrate upon the structure and dynamics of community and seek to answer the question: What is life like and how is it organized? The answer to this question is especially important for Chicanos where communities are attempting to resolve the problems of racism. Poplin maintained in the early 1970s that the above three types of studies were representative of community studies as a whole because they sought to understand the community in its totality. It is these types of studies that have lent insight into the nature and character of not only Chicanos but also other U.S. racial and ethnic people. However, these studies about Chicanos were slow in coming. Perhaps the best examples of early Anglo ethnographic studies are Robert S. and Helen M. Lynd's *Middletown: A Study of Contemporary American Culture* (1929) and *Middletown in Transition: A Study in Cultural Conflicts* (1937). In these studies the Lynds sought to understand the lifestyle of Middle Americans in a midwestern Indiana city just prior to the Great Depression. They concluded that American life proceeds upon the following activities: making a living, providing a home, training the young, using leisure time, practicing religion, and engaging in community activities. The Lynds strongly influenced the direction of my study of Bessemer (but not my conclusions) because they outlined areas of discrimination. Independently, other Chicano community researchers have discovered that the dynamics of racism and sexism are the same in other communities.

Chicano students at the time did not have the benefit of Chicano Studies programs. In fact, many of these 1960s and 1970s students founded and developed the discipline. These early scholars were concentrated in the social sciences, education, and modern languages. Chicanos in history, politics, sociology, economics, and anthropology took from their studies what was salient. They moved in a direction much different from the traditional disciplines to concentrate on prejudice and discrimination.

As mentioned above, early Chicano researchers did not find many Chicano rural communities to study. James West's (1945) research in Missouri provided insight into Anglo rural communities. It is an interesting contrast to the Lynds' Middletown studies and is within the ethnographic approach. My Bessemer community study (1990) incorporated some ethnographic techniques and areas of concentration, but it drew heavily on the work done between 1928 and 1967, when important ethnographic studies focused upon communities within larger communities. During my research the words "subcommunities" and "subcultures" appeared. I purposely did not, and do not, use these terms in order not to fall into the trap of extending the stereotype that Chicano communities are secondary, and thereby inferior, to other communities.

Several barrio studies were later motivated by Louis Wirth's *Ghetto* (1928), an in-depth study of African Americans in an urban setting. Herbert J. Gans published *Park Forest: The Birth of a Jewish Community* in 1951. This was followed by William Foote Whyte's famous study, *Street Corner Society* (1955), which concentrated on Italian males in Boston. In 1962, Gans returned with *Urban Villagers*, an outstanding discussion of Italian life in West Boston. In 1967 Elliot Leibow produced *Tally's Corner*, a study of African American male street life.

The above named studies were heavily influenced by the University of Chicago's school of sociological thought and the availability for study of northern and southern European immigrant communities founded in the late 19th and early 20th centuries. Chicanos were unlike these Europeans in that, contrary to traditional assumption, they were not immigrants and they did not have access to the vehicles of American upward mobility, even though they had been American citizens since 1848. My Bessemer study revealed that through conscious, and unconscious, decisions, they had not fully assimilated in 1978 in southern Colorado.

This lack of assimilation can be traced to the industrial beginning of the community of Bessemer. The community was, and is still, characterized by the Colorado Fuel and Iron Company (CF&I), the principal early employer of the region. The CF&I now belongs to a Nebraska firm, but it remains an important influence in Bessemer. Bessemer evolved much like other mining and steel-producing towns. In Arizona, mining communities were characterized by a substantial Chicano population. In the late 1970s Bessemer was reported to contain more than one-fourth of the Chicano population in Pueblo, which was about 43 percent Hispanic. This population has remained relatively stable even though the mill sharply reduced its 6,000-member work force in 1991. In 1978–1979, 2,095 of those workers were workers of color, and 1,934 were Chicano (Blea, 1991).

It is interesting to note the physical characteristics that shape the social character (personality) of the community. In Bessemer, the Bessemer Ditch, which fed into the Arkansas River was an important landmark. In all Chicano community studies the Mexican-U.S. border is important because of its symbolism. It, especially the Rio Grande, creates a dichotomy, a "we-they" (U.S.-Mexican) situation. The Arkansas River was once the northernmost border of Mexico and is fed by the Platte River. The CF&I and Bessemer are situated near what was once the northernmost boundary of the Nolan Land Grant. As in other Colorado communities, the Denver Rio Grande Railroad and the money and power of William J. Palmer and John D. Rockefeller, Jr., helped build Bessemer (Scamehorn, 1966). In a complex and interesting relationship the three came together in southern Colorado, seeking to profit by exploiting the extensive Santa Fe, New Mexico, trade. According to Scamehorn, they did not hire Mexicans until 1879, 11 years after northern Mexico became U.S. property.

A sociologist conducting research on the CF&I would find interesting—as part of the corporation's history—the existence of the Sociological Department within the company. Of greater interest is the impact that the department and the CF&I had, and still has, upon race/ethnic relations in the larger, culturally diverse ethnic community, with its large Mexican American population. The Sociological Department will be discussed later, but for now I will trace the development of class and color analysis in sociology.

CLASS AND COLOR ANALYSIS

The student of the Chicano community will find early class and color stratification studies in other communities documented in the field of sociology. Today, assimilation and acculturation studies are being conduced by such scholars as psychologist Judith Arroyo at the University of New Mexico. Preliminary, unpublished findings reveal that Chicanos are assimilating at varying rates, depending upon population concentration and their degree of urbanization.

Early studies placed emphasis upon social stratification and people of color. The best known early social stratification study was social anthropologist W. Lloyd Warner's *Yankee City* (1941). The most striking feature of this and other Warner studies is the exploration of white differences within a social system. August Hollingshead's *Elmtown's Youth* (1949) built on this work. Hollingshead found variances within classes of people in the same community. My Bessemer study revealed similar differences in the Chicano community. In other communities income levels are differentiated from class differences, and class differences deal with value differentials. In Bessemer, however, there was little value differential rooted in income variances. Expanding upon Hollingshead's work, Arthur Vidich and Joseph Bensman (1958) recognized that various groups of approximately equal social standing differed from one another in values and beliefs. This is more true of Chicanos than others but is made even more complex by the status and prestige allocated upon respect for age, knowledge, and history in the community.

Consistent with, yet different from social stratification studies, are race relations studies. It is in this area that Chicano community studies are concentrated. Scholars debate whether Chicanos should be considered a race or an ethnic group, a group of people with distinguishing ways of living. This way of living is different from the dominant culture and is frequently separated from it. Race, on the one hand, has to do with genetics and biology, ethnicity, on the other hand, has to do with culture. Generally, the discussion about where to place Chicanos is an Anglo exercise. This placement of people is in itself a cultural manifestation, and Chicanos have engaged in it. The characteristic gene pool that Anglos refer to when qualifying Chicanos as "racial minorities" is indigenous in nature. Chicanos are considered a racial group because they are mestizos, part American Indian and part European, and they are considered an ethnic group because they are European.

The early race and ethnic studies focused upon class, but also made clear the concept of caste: a concept based upon a discrimination process rooted in color, race, and, often, ethnicity that cements or limits social mobility. John Dollard's *Caste and Class in a Southern Town* (1937) and Allison Davis and Burleigh and Mary Gardner's *Deep South* (1941) gave insight into the social mechanisms that produced subordinate-dominant relations between African Americans and whites in the south. That Chicano Studies adopted some of these concepts is evident in early Chicano Studies.

During the 1970s most white stratification researchers omitted the very important discussion of caste. According to Allison Davis, however, rural caste was organized around the control of gender and sexual activity. The premise was that white males had easy access to African American females during the slavery period, but white females did not have equal access to black males. Thus, white males controlled white female sexuality and imposed themselves on black females, while black males could have sex only with black women. The black male population not only had no sexual access to the white population, but it was also relegated to lower-class and lower-color caste positions that were inescapable. Unlike white ethnics who could climb out of lower-class positions, African Americans could not. They could not escape the fact that their skin was obviously dark, and that they were discriminated against because of it. The same holds true for Chicanos today although caste is rarely referred to in sexual terms. Mario Barrera (1979) first introduced the concept of caste in Chicano Studies. This tradition of American black-white race relations continued after slavery ended, and the United States expanded westward and its citizens encountered other people of color (American Indians and Mexicans.) All Americans now live with this social inheritance.

Of specific interest in Davis's community study is its focus upon sexual politics. This is one of the first academic works to emphasize the intersection of gender and race. Until this appeared, gender (especially the role of women of color) was not a high area of interest in the male-dominated field of race and ethnic relations. Since then, however, studies of women of color have been published, and it has become a very important area of concentration, contributing heavily to the paradigm shift, the way academics think about the nature of society in the social sciences.

To test the concept of caste in an urban setting, in the mid 1940s, W. Lloyd Warner assisted in directing Sinclair Drake and Horace Cayton's *Black Metropolis* (1945), a study of the lives of African Americans in Chicago. Unlike *Deep South*, or *Middletown*, the study did not focus upon the lifestyle of the white population and how they lived with racism. Instead, Drake and Cayton's emphasis was more holistic. They drew from economics, politics, migration, and the upper, lower, and middle classes to render an analysis of the quality of life for African Americans. This study concluded that caste was germane to rural life but that it also existed in the city. African Americans were more trapped in the lower class than white people because of their color. This appears to be the first true analysis of the intersection of race and class. Intersection and the intersection of variables, in this text, mean the coming together, crossing, or mixing of two or more variables or factors to produce specific behavior.

RACE RELATIONS

The review of the literature reveals that discrimination is pervasive, historical, and rooted into the American psyche as part of the country's national heritage. In the United States, race relations has historically been considered as consisting of negative white-black relations; but it is important to remember that most ethnic or racial groups have experienced discrimination regardless of color. Some groups have escaped the trappings of discrimination, especially those groups that are white. Some, particularly groups of color, have not escaped it, even when they want to assimilate, be absorbed, or be incorporated into the dominant group. Rarely are positive race relations documented.

Most Chicano scholars hope for better race relations between Anglos and raza, the people of Latino heritage. When Chicano movement activists turned into academics in the 1960s and 1970s, they did so to foster better relations, but mostly to empower the raza. These academics continued their activism both in the classroom and in the community. In fact, even today classroom activities are considered activism. They are a valuable part of the community as they represent the intellegencia of the community. It was only when this group of Chicano movement activists entered higher education that several Chicano Studies Departments appeared and that some Chicano community studies were initiated. But, other factors also influenced the nature of community studies: ex-president Lyndon B. Johnson's War on Poverty, criticism and resistance to the Vietnam War, the hippie movement, the women's movement.

The War on Poverty certainly influenced Chicano Studies but so did the continued work of other academics who had experienced the social upheaval of the 1960s. David Schulz (1969), in an ethnographic tradition, paid close attention to African American urban ghetto life in the heart of St. Louis. His focus upon growing up African American in a housing project discusses the life process of birth through old age in complete and incomplete families. My Bessemer study exhibits some of Schulz's methodology. There are problems, however, with his family categories because they imply that a complete nuclear family is a more legitimate form of family and that incomplete families (single-parent families) are not really families, but deviants from the normal state. Schulz focuses upon that which was most deviant from mainstream society, and thus he has a tendency to view African American urban life as deviant. This tendency to cast people of color as deviants has affected the analysis of both the African American and the Chicano social experience.

Chicano poverty and lack of educational attainment were subjects of Chicano research in the 1960s, but they were over-ridden by focus upon history. Chicano history was generally excluded from academic study at every level of education. The Anglo proclivity to stereotype and study Chicanos as some form of deviance extended into the 1970s. Non-Chicano researchers tended to study drug addiction, urban gangs, curanderismo, and dysfunctional Mexican families. It was not until academicians of color and women entered the field that these tendencies were tempered.

The areas upon which 1960s scholars concentrated are of great interest to the student of Chicano communities. These areas included class and racial discrimination—how they intersected, and how this deterred attainment of political power, employment, health care, quality housing, and upward mobility. Today, study in all the areas have been expanded to include gender. Nevertheless, the 1960s activism gave true direction to the interdisciplinary perspective. This perspective draws from various academic fields to paint a more accurate picture of people of color. It emerged primarily out of the need to respond to poor and culturally biased Anglo research.

Two studies that incurred special critique were Ruth Tuck's *Not with the Fist* (1946) and Lyle Saunder's *Cultural Differences and Medical Care of the Spanish Speaking People in the Southwest* (1954). These are not community studies but fall, instead, into a category described in Poplin (1972) as "the community as an independent variable." They treat the community as an influencing factor and do not shed much light upon everyday life. Social scientists conducting these studies were more interested in the dependent variable than in the community. They assumed that a change in one variable causes a change in another. Thus, community size influences fertility, attitudes, and values. Although these studies do not lend insight into quality of life or life's processes, they may assist in understanding community change.

In keeping with the treatment of the community as an independent variable, some researchers have linked low academic achievement by Chicanos to the population's cultural characteristics. Studies by Audrey Schwartz and C. Wayne Gordon are reviewed in Deluvina Hernandez's monograph *Mexican American Challenge to a Sacred Cow* (1970). In one study Schwartz stereotypically asserts that Mexican Americans seek immediate gratification through manipulative, expressive behavior and through emphasis on scheming. This comparative study establishes Chicanos as abnormal or ineffective in their behavior. Schwartz and Gordon conclude in a second study that the root of low achievement by Mexican American youth is found in the culture that is transmitted by the family. The Chicanos' problems can be solved by assimilation, moving away from family influence and the culture that inhibits achievement. Chicago social scientists have highly criticized this work. The first such criticism came from Octavio Romano in "The Anthropology and Sociology of the Mexican Americans: The Distortion of Mexican American History" (1968). Other highly criticized works include studies by Florence Kluckhohn and Fred Strodbeck (1961), Celia Heller (1966), William Medsen (1964), Julian Samora and Richard Lamanna (1967), plus the already mentioned studies by Tuck and Saunders.

The Chicano interdisciplinary perspective was given direction by Chicano social scientists who were social activists. Early in the development of the field, the field was dominated by men. Chicano male academics clustered in disciplines that included a combination of history and political science. Some early works of Chicano scholars include those of Carlos Munoz (1972), Raymond A. Roco (1976), Rodolpho Acuna (1972, 1981), and Mario Barrera (1979). Males dominated the field, but not for long. Chicanas began to confront male dominance in the mid 1970s. In the 1980s they began to get published and by the 1990s there were a considerable number of works by Chicanas available.

INTERNAL COLONIALISM

African Americans have a somewhat longer tradition than Chicanos of focusing upon their own social conditions. This in part is due to the existence of African American scholars in predominantly African American universities who were able to provide a valuable base for a very critical analysis of American society. Chicanos and Chicanas, on the other hand, had minuscule university experience. While Chicanos did draw from this activist scholarship for motivation, Chicano scholarship has been fashioned more after the works of Frantz Fanon (1963), Albert Memmi (1965), and Karl Marx (1848), who provided a class analysis. Since Chicano barrios were filled with people of color, its study has been more heavily influenced by caste and color analysis. Nevertheless, remnants of these early divisions can still be felt. When women entered the field, Chicano community research took on another dimension, one more concerned with the daily lives of people.

As has been discussed, Chicano social scientists reacted to theoretical models that were in place when they arrived on the academic scene. In response to the dysfunctional "Chicanos as abnormal" or "deviant" models, Chicanos developed the theory of internal colonialism. Internal colonialism has dominated the study of Chicanos for over 20 years. I tested its applicability to the Bessemer experience and found it useful, but it was not sufficient to explain the dynamics of sexism and other aspects that I discovered. I would recommend that a student of the Chicano community conduct a similar test in order to establish not only the saliency of the model, but also to promote new knowledge.

Internal colonialism will be discussed further in the chapters on theoretical development. For now the student should know that it incorporates various elements of race relations theories. Its emphasis in Chicano studies began with Robert Blauner's internal colonial perspective (1969, 1972), which maintains that racial prejudice is largely a product of racial ideologies that were developed to justify structural discrimination. In other words, racist behavior exists because racist thoughts and beliefs are held and these beliefs justify the behaviors that work to exclude certain people. The most obvious example exists in employment. Job competition between Anglos and people of color increases racial tension and prejudice, and sometimes violence. Internal colonialism is rooted in historical violence, and it exists in the current society in order to maintain Anglo dominance. It starts when one group conquers (forcefully subjugates) another and continues to maintain dominance by securing the conquered's labor power, their land and other resources. Specifics of the conquest include not only the appropriation of very cheap labor power, but also their water, plants, trees, animals, air, and air space. In my opinion, the conquest is most complete when labor power is dependent upon the dominant structure and the physical environment that sustained the conquered population has been brought under control, polluted, and/or destroyed. Internal colonialism maintains that the dominant and subordinate populations give the appearance of being intermingled, but distinctive differences in quality of life are highly apparent. The outward appearance that equality reigns keeps most of the conquered striving to achieve what the conqueror possesses.

The internal colonial model has revealed the social reality to Chicanos. The "conquered" generally exists within the larger compound of a city or state, and people of both the dominant and subordinate group must interrelate; but a physically segregated space, with a name, is marked as social space for raza. Relationships are generally limited to specific interactions, such as the exchange of money for purchases and the delivery of services. The degree of controlled interaction varies according to social history and population density. Where raza are very, very small in number they may not encounter the same kind of discrimination that is experienced by populations that are larger.

The historical relationship of subordination coincides with regional population concentration, but an essential feature of internal colonialism is systematic discrimination. Carlos Munoz (1972) maintains that dominant-minority relations are not only characterized by racism, but that the cultural minority comprises a "third world" within the internal boundaries of the United States. This perspective postulates that the dominant culture believes that Chicanos have entered into a governing relationship with the Anglo on an involuntary basis. This is not true. The relationship is characterized by conflict. It began with military conflict (the U.S. war with Mexico) and has been maintained through conflict and police force. A critical and distinguishing factor in internal colonialism is the legal status of the colonized. A colony is characterized as internal if the population has the same formal status as any other group. Chicanos constitute an internal colony because they are legal citizens occupying a status of formal equality, although informally their status is one of inequality.

A system of dominance evolves over time, and it changes with the times. This is most visible in the U.S. Indian reservation system, but it is also apparent in the cities with regard to people of color. In his Chicano community study Alberto Camarillo (1979) documented the creation of a California barrio as a historical procedure of deterioration, economic control, and racial discrimination. The same is true for Bessemer. It underwent this process, but unlike the barrio studied by Camarillo, the nature and character of it was strongly defined by Colorado Fuel & Iron's Sociological Department, a department that strove to control the behavior of the workers and their families.

The objective of the department was to shape an ethnically diverse population into one with common values and social norms. It had a plan designed to fulfill the official aim of the company: to produce a homogeneous working body that would arrive at work on time, work a full shift, go home, rest, and arise to work again. This cycle was repeated when the workers' families returned the company's revenue by shopping at the company store. From its conception, as in the Camarilllo study, Bessemer has been (and continues to be in many ways) a community distinct from the larger Pueblo community.

Contemporary Chicano communities seek to liberate themselves from colonial forces. Liberation includes resistance to the internalization of dominant values and freedom and emancipation from racism and sexism, as well as cultural sovereignty. Cultural sovereignty calls for the cultural integrity and the dignity of a people to be recognized and respected. Chicanos have demanded that the authority behind the Treaty of Guadalupe Hidalgo be recognized, that they be incorporated as viable participants into the U.S. dominion; but for some it means that they retain supremacy, or jurisdiction, over land once occupied by them and their Indian ancestors.

Chicano liberation from Anglo social entrapment and intimidation involves developing group consciousness and rejecting established Anglo conditions. It means that Chicanos must decolonize, do away with colonization. Colonization hurts Indians and Chicanos, and it hurts society as a whole because it is an outdated form of governing. It costs the society resources in the form of unrealized talent, skills, international legitimacy, and money.

CHICANA STUDIES

Activist Chicanas addressed some of the above outlined concerns in their communities and on university and college campuses in the 1960s and 1970s. Their scholarship grew with their increased involvement on campuses. This advancement in scholarship is outlined in another chapter, but for now it is sufficient to note that the struggle against oppression in Chicano communities has taken a multifaceted approach. In one aspect Chicana scholarship has adopted a third world perspective that actively criticizes the society in which Chicanos are forced to exist. Chicana feminist criticism also analyzes power relationships at the national and international levels. It frequently identifies itself with the struggles of third world countries because Chicana feminists believe Chicano communities are colonized communities caught in secondary power relations to the dominant community. This situation is similar to that of disempowered countries and their relationships to the United States.

Chicana scholarship is very much within the mainstream of Chicano Studies. Women's Studies and more traditional disciplines are now paying attention to this work. Although it is gaining some acceptance, it was initially considered deviant from established, acceptable, scholarship because it was critical of male-dominant, middle-class, Anglo (white) paradigms. The Chicana focus upon the role of women, family, religion, and sexism is stretching, deleting, adjusting, and ultimately changing the dominant, customary way of thinking and doing things, not only in academia but also in Chicano communities.

There are basically two ways for the student to enter the field after the review of literature has taken place: armed with a hypothesis or unarmed, searching for a grounded theory. Grounded theory will be more thoroughly discussed in the next chapter. It is most important that the student review the literature before entering the field and that the student protect herself/himself from potential overload and biases that have more to do with the American cultural inheritance of prejudice and discrimination than with social science. To prevent this, the review should be analyzed and categorized into different schools of thought, much as is done in this chapter. The student should keep in mind that expanding her/his knowledge is a cycle of exploration in which there is a symbiotic relationship between conducting research and the formulation of theory based upon that research. Therefore, methodology, how research is conducted is important. The student can begin investigation by conducting research (induction) or by testing a theory (deduction) that was developed based upon research. Crucial to the broadest, most consensual way of thinking and doing things (paradigm) is the Chicano Studies analysis of the intersection of variables: the place where race, class, and gender converge, meet, to impact the nature of the community. Most important, behavior is slowly changing. Chicanas are forcing a change in men, a change in the family, and a change in academia. As this academic force gains national and international attention, the direction of scholarship (especially that reflecting the analysis of women of color) is also transforming knowledge about the nature of communities, human beings, and social forces.

REFERENCES

Acuna, Rodolpho. 1972. *Occupied America: The Struggle Toward Chicano Liberation.* San Francisco: Canfield Press.

———. 1981. *Occupied America: A History of Chicanos.* San Francisco: Harper and Row. 2d ed. of *Occupied America* (1972).

Barrera, Mario. 1979. *Race and Class in the Southwest*. Notre Dame: University of Notre Dame Press.

Blauner, Robert. 1969. "Internal Colonialism and Ghetto Revolt." *Social Problems*, 16 (Spring): 393–408.

———. 1972. *Racial Oppression in America*. New York: Harper and Row.

Blea, Irene I. 1991. *Bessemer: A Sociological Perspective of a Chicano Barrio*. New York: AMS Press.

Camarillo, Alberto. 1979. *Chicanas in a Changing Society*. Cambridge: Harvard University Press.

Davis, Allison, Burleigh B. Gardner, and Mary R. Gardner. 1941. *Deep South*. Chicago: University of Chicago Press.

Dollard, John. 1937. *Caste and Class in a Southern Town*. New Haven: Yale University Press.

Drake, Sinclair, and Horace Cayton. 1945. *Black Metropolis*. New York: Harcourt, Brace and World, Inc.

Fanon, Frantz. 1963. *The Wretched of the Earth*. New York: Grove Press.

Gans, Herbert J. 1951. "Park Forest: Birth of a Jewish Community." *Commentary*, vol. 11.

———. 1962. *The Urban Villagers*. New York: The Free Press.

Heller, Celia. 1966. *Mexican American Youth: Forgotten Youth at the Crossroads*. New York: Random House.

Hernandez, Deluvina. 1970. *Mexican American Challenge to a Sacred Cow*. Los Angeles: Chicano Cultural Center.

Hollingshead, August B. 1949. *Elmtown's Youth*. New York: John Wiley and Sons, Inc.

Kluckhohn, Florence, and Fred L. Strodbeck. 1961. *Variations in Value Orientations*. Evanston, Ill.: Raw Peterson.

Leibow, Elliot. 1967. *Tally's Corner: A Study of Negro Streetcorner Men*. Boston: Little, Brown and Company.

Lynd, Robert S., and Helen M. Lynd. 1929. *Middletown: A Study of Contemporary American Culture*. New York: Harcourt, Brace.

———. 1937. *Middletown in Transition: A Study in Cultural Conflicts*. New York: Harcourt, Brace.

Marx, Karl, and Friedrich Engels. 1964. *Communist Manifesto*. In Arthur Mendel, ed., *Essential Works of Marxism*, pp. 13–44. New York: Bantam Books. Originally published in 1848.

Medsen, William. 1964. *Mexican Americans of South Texas*. New York: Holt, Rinehart and Winston.

Memmi, Albert. 1965. *The Colonizer and the Colonized*. Boston: Beacon Press.

Munoz, Carlos J. 1972. *The Politics of Urban Protest: A Model of Political Analysis*. Claremont, Calif.: Claremont Graduate School of Government.

Nisbet, Robert A. 1962. *Community and Power: A Study in the Ethics of Order and Freedom*. New York: Oxford University Press.

Poplin, Dennis E. 1972. *Communities: A Survey of Theories and Methods of Research*. New York: Macmillan Publishing Co., Inc.

Roco, Raymond A. 1976. "The Chicano in Social Sciences: Traditional Concepts, Myths and Images." *Aztlan: International Journal of Chicano Studies* (Spring). Los Angeles: Chicano Cultural Center.

Romano, Octavio. 1968. "The Anthropology and Sociology of the Mexican Americans: The Distortion of Mexican-American History." *El Grito* (Fall).

Samora, Julian, and Richard A. Lamanna. 1967. *Mexican Americans in a Midwest Metropolis: A Study of East Chicago*. Los Angeles: Mexican American Project.

Saunders, Lyle. 1954. *Cultural Differences and Medical Care of the Spanish Speaking People in the Southwest*. New York: Russell Sage Foundation.

Scamehorn, H. Lee. 1966. *Pioneer Steelmakers in the West*. Boulder, Colo.: Pruett Publishing Company.

Schulz, David A. 1969. *Coming Up African American: Patterns of Ghetto Socialization*. Englewood Cliff, N.J.: Prentice-Hall, Inc.

Tuck, Ruth. 1946. *Not with the Fist: Mexican Americans in a Southwest City*. New York: Harcourt, Brace and Company.

Vidich, Arthur J., and Joseph Bensman. 1958. *Small Town in Mass Society*. Princeton, New Jersey: Princetown University Press.

Warner, W. Lloyd. 1941. *Yankee City*. New Haven: Yale University Press.

Warner, W. Lloyd, and Paul S. Lunt. 1941. *The Social Life of a Modern Community*. New Haven: Yale University Press.

———. 1942. *The Status System of a Modern Community*. New Haven: Yale University Press.

Warner, W. Lloyd, et al. 1949. *Democracy in Jonesville*. New York: Harper and Row.

West, James. 1945. *Plainville, U.S.A.* New York: Columbia University Press.

Wirth, Louis. 1928. *The Ghetto*. Chicago: University of Chicago Press.

Whyte, William Foote. 1955. *Street Corner Society*. Chicago: University of Chicago Press.

Models posing for a beauty salon and spa.

3 Methodology and the Study of Racial and Ethnic Communities

This chapter furthers the student's understanding of the research process by introducing the student to research methodology, the procedure used when conducting research. An important element of this chapter is its focus on cultural values and how they affect the research process. The chapter also sets the basis for an understanding of the theory that explains why what is happening is happening in the way in which it is happening. Theory is used to establish generalizations about the community and will be discussed in depth in a later chapter.

Studying the Chicano community requires some rethinking of how community living conditions are conceptualized and explained. Chicano community studies are squarely placed within the context of Chicano Studies and the interdisciplinary development of that academic unit. As mentioned in the preceding chapters, much of the early work in Chicano Studies was reactionary; it reacted to what was considered to be the injustices by non-Chicano academics. This phase quickly evolved into an alternative perspective on behalf of Chicanos that caused social scientists to either change or adjust their worldview. Chicanos empowered themselves with the tools of research and presented the Chicano condition through Chicano eyes. This reassessment has evolved to the point where Chicano scholars no longer attempt to build sensitivity for the victims of Anglo injustice. Instead, they very assertively extend their perspectives and challenge others to test it.

This challenge is part of the role of science. Social scientists extend their perspectives based on data and allow their colleagues to react to it in journals and at conferences. Once this process is complete, the research becomes part of the general literature on the subject and may be included in another scholar's literature review.

THE NATURE OF RESEARCH

When Chicano communities were first being studied by non-Chicanos, the concentration was upon what was wrong with them. Chicano academics extended perspective and explained what appeared to be dysfunctional from an insider's perspective. The topics of research included much focus upon education, asserting that school "drop out" rates were "push out" rates. In short, the schools were ineffective in teaching Chicano youth and pushed them out of school. Drug use and gang activity were examined for how they met group needs. Politics, the healing tradition of curanderismo, and the lives of family developed as areas of concentration. Minimal effort was placed on studying the elderly, until more recently when funding sources became available because of the aging U.S. population.

Conducting research includes not only delving into what has happened in the past, but also finding funding for the research project. Most Chicanos have conducted research with little or no funding in the name of "the cause," in an attempt to empower the community and to maintain employment. Most academics find funding for research through their institutions or by soliciting funding from various sources in the form of grants. Writing grants is time consuming and was often riddled with racism and sexism that exhibited itself in the types of projects announced for funding and in the selection process. Some Chicanos have been able to participate in major studies by allying themselves with Anglo researchers.

The studies conducted are either quantitative or qualitative. Quantitative studies are usually statistical studies. Exponential smoothing and multiple linear regression analysis are examples that reflect quantitative approaches to studying something. They can be used to forecast educational or demographic rates, thereby explaining what is likely to happen over a course of time. Qualitative studies are rooted in questions that have to do with the quality or condition of life. The kinds of questions asked may dictate what kind of research design is required and what kind of measurement instruments will be used to collect data. Measurement instruments include the survey, the written response questionnaire, observation, and the interview that document oral and behavioral responses.

To make predictions the scholar must gather data. Put very simply, data are a series of facts used to establish a conclusion. How the facts are gathered, the methodology, is important because the method has much to do with the outcome of the study. Methodology sets the parameters in which the study takes place, and if the parameters are culturally biased or inappropriately defined, the findings may be biased or false.

Gathering data is time consuming. It leads to analyzing, making sense out of the findings and establishing generalizations, or drawing conclusions. This is a complex task requiring specific training. Before the advent of computers this phase was highly labor intensive. While conducting the research for Bessemer, I had no access to computers. Everything, including the typing, had to be done manually. Chicanos were among the last to gain computer access.

CULTURAL VALUES

When designing and conducting research in the Chicano community, it is important that the respondents' cultural and social history and values be observed and respected. Failure to do this may bias the research. Gerardo Marin and Barbara VanOss Marin (1991) give a simplified summary of basic Hispano cultural values, but I found it to be too Eurocentric. Their areas of concentration, their categories, are the Anglo male and are dominated by academia. The authors claim that Hispanos are allocentric, rooted in collectivism. This term is anthropological and ignores the complexity of holistic approaches to life. A more holistic, interdisciplinary approach is advised. Allocentric societies emphasize the needs, the objectives, and the points of view of the group, while individualistic cultures determine their social behavior primarily in terms of personal objectives. This dichotomy does not take into consideration that contemporary Chicanos are tricultural; they have indigenous, Mexicano, and Americano cultural values that they employ selectively. Further, Chicanos have not all developed at the same time in the same direction. Although Marin and VanOss Marin recognize some diversity among Hispanos, they posit that the European aspect of Latino culture is in direct contrast with dominant Anglo culture, and they totally neglect an in-depth discussion of the intersection of class, region, race, and gender differences. Marin shares authorship with H.G. Triandis (1985) to propose that allocentrism is associated with personal interdependence, field sensitivity, conformity, mutual empathy, willingness to sacrifice for the welfare of the in-group, and trust of the members of the in-group. They do not discuss how this is being threatened by drugs and gangs or abandoned by the upwardly mobile in favor of assimilation. In general, however, scholars agreed that Marin and VanOss Marin are correct in maintaining that Hispanos prefer interpersonal relationships within the in-group that are nurturing, loving, intimate, and respectful, but a historical and regional context is missing. Traditionally, there was more egalitarianism between gender and age categories; but this is being highly threatened in the 1990s. Chicanos do tend to demonstrate a certain level of conformity and empathy for the feelings of others, but this is not always true, especially in large urban areas. Chicanos certainly will not act this way with Anglo researchers.

This tendency toward more integrated interpersonal relationships can be of significance in conducting research with Chicanos, not because it makes explicitly clear the need for friendly interactions between researcher and respondent, but because positive Chicano relationships require respect. Especially with the elderly, this need to integrate personal relationships may lead to the respondent providing socially desirable answers. It is not so much that respondents lie, but that they may be striving for acceptance or social harmony. If they dislike the researcher, they may lie. If they do not know the answer or if they are trying to think like the researcher, they may stretch the truth. These factors, however, can describe any group of respondents. Marin and VanOss Marin maintain that Chicano respondents acquiesce. This is an elitist viewpoint and demonstrates the hierarchical thinking that permeates Anglo thought processes. The term *"simpatia"* more closely describes what is happening. The Hispano cultural script is more derived from emphases on the need for behavior that promotes smooth, pleasant, social relationships. The majority of Chicanos expect to encounter discrimination or belittlement from those in powerful positions. Most Chicanas expect sexism and racism. This is not solely attitude; it is a result of social conditioning. If Anglo researchers can expect anything, they can expect something related to the Hawthorn effect: that Chicanos will render what they think the Anglo researcher wants to hear so that she/he will go away.

The most important point is that researchers need not establish a positive relationship with Hispano respondents in order to get the best results; instead, they need to demonstrate respect. Because Hispanos have been victimized, they may fall into the classic victim syndrome. Researchers, especially Anglo researchers, must allow for more intense research because they do not know how to set boundaries. For the researcher to manipulate a friendship is unprofessional. The researcher exploits the respondent's emotions and severely disrupts the validity and reliability of the methodology, even the data, its analysis, and conclusions.

Marin and VanOss Marin make a good point in asserting that more talk, casual conversation, is required when working with Chicano subjects. This is part of the Chicano social process, and is especially imperative when conducting qualitative studies. If coffee or cake is offered to the researcher by the subject, it is recommended that it be accepted. Sometimes the respondent went to special effort to supply it, and it may be reciprocity for the attention on the "visit." Researchers can expect such offerings from older people but not always from more youthful respondents. It would be more likely that the researcher would encounter shyness among the younger respondents.

Familialism is one of the most important Chicano cultural variables. This value needs to be combined with an understanding of the desires and expectations of families and the desires and expectations of individuals within families. Some of these desires include a better quality of life for the family, a healthy family, an extended family, a strong feeling of loyalty to the home, the house which shelters the family. Reciprocity and solidarity among members of the same family are expected but the researcher should not be surprised to find them missing. The contention that the family is important needs to be placed within the context that it is used selectively. Traditionally the family has been expected to protect against physical harm and the emotional stress of coping with discrimination (Grebler, Moore, and Guzman, 1970; Mannino and Shore, 1976; Cohen, 1979; Valle and Martinez, 1980), but it is now subjected to various other stresses and is rapidly changing. Familialism has traditionally included an obligation to provide material and emotional support, but, like in other U.S. families, the global and domestic economy no long make this possible. In addition, the Angloization of Mexican Americans has placed an emphasis on individualism, and not all Chicanos worry about how they are perceived by the family, relatives, neighbors, and *compadres* and *comadres*, the spiritual family members. Thus, the researcher must delineate what social factors are functioning to define family interaction and is advised not to manipulate or appeal to family values. To do this is to stereotype Chicanos, thus biasing the conclusions.

Further, there should be no incentives, such as small gifts to children or relatives, to motivate respondents to participate in research. This reeks of the "white man" attempting to cheat the Indian. If compensation is offered, it should be discussed at the onset, should be consistently awarded among all respondents, and should come in a form that compensates for time at the market value of compensation for respondents in other research projects. If no compensation is tendered, it is culturally appropriate to reciprocate by contributing to the community in the form of rendering research findings in print, in lectures at community meetings, and/or advocating for the community.

Another stereotype generally held by researchers is that Hispanics do not need as much physical space as others. In the recent past there was some indication that Latinos needed less personal space than Anglos, but this has not been tested for over 25 years, and it may no longer be true. In fact, I contend that the more assimilated or acculturated the respondent is to the Anglo culture, the more space she/he demands. Non-Hispanos who prefer to stand further apart than Latinos may find themselves uncomfortable with individuals who may be unconsciously angry at Anglos for allowing discrimination to exist among their people. When Chicanos do not fulfill the Anglo stereotype, Anglos may think them "pushy" or "impolite" or "distant" because they are not staying in their place. Anglos need to understand that Chicanos see them as one race with little distinction of the cultural differences found among whites.

Another stereotype is that there is a difference in time orientation among Mexican Americans. This also must be researched. Over the past 25 years Hispanos, professional Chicanos, and bicultural Latinos have worked to be on time in order to escape this dangerous stereotype. The "mañana" syndrome is not only a stereotype, it is effective in establishing the Chicano as lazy, ineffectual, and incompetent. Lateness may have more to do with a busy life, transportation problems, and/or resistance to Anglos.

The researcher must also be aware of gender roles. Men may not want to have family and "significant other" females participate in a study. Unsolicited attention is discussed and is consistent with sexism and control of women. It is especially seen among families with higher education where fathers, brothers, boyfriends, and husbands often do not want women to change. They monitor female time away from home. The effect upon research is that women may feel uncomfortable talking, especially about gender issues, with "significant other" males present, including Anglo males.

Contrary to popular belief, Latinos place a high value in education. They believe it provides upward mobility and job training. Very few value education for the accumulation and distribution of knowledge. Learning as a life long endeavor, as valued in Anglo households, is rarely discussed. Even though a few families have professors and other scientists as members of the family, most Latinos have not discussed research. Thus, conducting research is not a career option.

For Chicanos interested in research there is another factor at play: the quality of education afforded Chicanos, both through the curriculum and the environment in which education takes place. Unlike this generation, the first generation of Chicano academics did not have the benefit of groups of people interested in supporting students. To put it simply, Chicanos were not going to college in the 1960s, 1970s, and into the mid 1980s, and the goal was to get them onto college and university campuses and to graduate them. The issue was access. A few succeeded. This issue remained into the 1990s, when concentrated efforts were made to get students into the math and science fields in order to stimulate more quantitative studies.

ACTIVIST SCHOLARSHIP

Much of the work done on Chicano communities still focuses upon the dysfunctional, the deviant, elements of the Chicano experience (gangs, drug addiction, HIV). Not much is being done to counteract this. In fact, Chicano scholars are writing books about it. It has been suggested that those researching the community also frame their work within the context of "survival or coping mechanisms," ask themselves what is good, positive, functional, and optimistic, and outline these as areas for analysis. This trend would produce activist scholarship and would help to break the stereotypes. For this to happen a qualitative approach is helpful because it requires intensive interviewing or talking, *platica*, in order to get to the intricacies of the reality of life. It has been suggested that Chicanas, for example, cope very well and some even overachieve; but how they attain this high standard has not been systematically documented.

I believe that they do so because they know they have to or they will suffer poverty. Also, oppression can produce creativity. Those who have started with a dream may have chosen not to listen to those who are negative. No one may be available to help them when they approach the unapproachable. They may draw upon their culture to network and select friends who have sifted through the complexity of their own lives. They do not give up. Everyday they have reason to quit, but if they quit, too much goes wrong. Some may even have learned to value themselves. Perhaps they know that if they stop once, they will stop forever, that they represent their people and cannot fail. They may love their people and their culture. They may be willing to work at whatever it takes to get through life. They may have role models and/or a history of helping others fulfill their dreams. Maybe, they dare to dream in the first place. If they can conceive it, they can do it because they have learned not to be afraid or ashamed of the passions they feel for what they want to do.

Does documenting the functional bias a scientific analysis? It biases a study to the degree that making a choice about what to study is a bias and is, therefore, inherent to the research process. At the time that a researcher selects a topic to examine all other possible choices are excluded. For this reason not only has "value free" science become an issue but Chicano Studies has also become a political issue on college and university campuses. There were, and are, individuals who do not want Chicana or Chicano Studies taught on campus. This causes organizational and policy push, pull, and shoving and results in political camps and negative relationships among scholars. There are even some activists who contend that everything we do is political. A choice has consequences because these consequences manifest as social impacts. If enough people make the same choice, then a social trend is established. If the trend continues, then a social fact is established. It is for this reason that every individual is important. For example, not acting on the issues of women has a social consequence; choosing not to act is still an action and renders an unhealthy lifestyle for women. People choosing not to act may also be implying that women or they, themselves, are not important enough to be given serious consideration.

Academics opting to do Chicano research and to disseminate this knowledge in Chicano Studies classes, professional journals, book publications, and to the Chicano community make some definite choices. Because they choose not to isolate themselves on campus, their colleagues may think they are unprofessional and more concerned with politics. Much campus pressure—to publish, to serve on committees—is placed upon the Chicano activist scholar to keep ideas in the classroom by traditional scholars. Since most Chicano scholars teach in predominantly Anglo institutions and their students rarely venture into Chicano communities, this defeats the entire purpose of specializing in Chicano Studies, where emphasis is placed upon applied research.

It is not easy for Chicana and Chicano academicians to publish. They are competing with thousands of other academics and there are only limited avenues of publication. Articles are more frequently published than books, and book-publishing firms are highly interested in how much profit can be made from the sale of a book. Many good manuscripts are rejected only because the publishing firm has decided that the manuscript market, the expected profit, is too limited. In addition, publishes may have either accepted the stereotype of the illiterate Mexican or they may not have ventured to study and develop the existing market.

The student has already been advised that reviewing the literature will assist in defining the research project. The literature that will be reviewed is that which has been outlined above. Seeking to expand this literature is seen as revolutionary or an act of reform. It is for this reason that Chicano scholars are still seen as more interested in politics and as part of the on-going and constantly changing Chicano Movement.

Even after 25 years of Chicano Studies, an entirely new generation of Chicano activist academics are still seen as rebels or as heavily linked to streetwise revolutionaries (Frammolino, 1993). Early activist scholars now have grandchildren. Some Chicano students have beepers and cellular phones, but they still had to stage sit-ins and go on hunger strikes at UCLA because they wanted a Chicano Studies Department and the institution was resisting. Journalists still write about how Chicano students want respect and want to learn more about themselves and their people's experience in the United States (Frammolino, 1993). This is important because students are still learning in hierarchical fashion the Anglo version of the foundation and formulation of the country. They are still taught in English from a male-dominated perspective. In summary, they are still in a sexist, Eurocentric, Anglo-dominated system that degrades and ignores entire indigenous civilizations and Mexican contributions.

A generation of students grew up with bilingual classes being constantly threatened by the Nixon, Reagan and Bush administrations. Only meager resources were available for ethnic awareness programs and cultural holiday celebrations on campus during the cruel Republican years. This generation knows the system has the potential to design programs to meet their needs, and they want those needs met. Today there are more Latinos going to college. In the University of California system alone, Latino enrollment has more than doubled between 1981 to 1992 (from 5.9 percent to 13.1 percent) (Frammolino, 1993). More students are making their painful way through grammar and high schools around the country. The percentage of Latino students in high school was 23 percent in 1980 but is expected to balloon to 41 percent in 2010. Many U.S. born Latino students still arrive on campus searching for their roots. Many immigrants come searching for a way to escape the trappings of the discrimination they have inherited. Many still drop out. Latinos have the lowest graduation rate of any ethnic group.

Other issues also exist on campuses around the country. Students have protested the serving of grapes at institutions. The Boycott Grapes campaign of the United Farm Workers targets the use of pesticides on the nation's fruit. University and college students are tied to community issues and note that only the nature of oppression in the fields has changed since Cesar Chavez and the farm workers linked with students and the general community to boycott grapes over 25 years ago. Today university and college campuses have Cesar Chavez centers. Who teaches and administers these centers has become a student, community, and faculty issue.

In the University of California system, the largest in the nation, Latinos still make up only 4 percent of the faculty. On most U.S. campuses this figure is lower. California State University in Los Angeles has the oldest Chicano Studies Department in the nation as well as the largest percentage of Chicano students; but it has only increased its share of faculty from 4.8 percent in 1990 to 5.3 percent 1994, well below the 43 percent Latino student population enrolled on that campus.

The Chicano presence on campuses supports the research process. Basically, research centers upon a question the researcher seeks to answer. Most students are taught to pose hypotheses, statements about the expected relationship between variables. They are asked to identify variables and characteristics that vary from one group or individual to the next. Chicano scholars generally prefer grounded research that is rooted in the Chicano experience and rendered by those who have had that experience.

A hypothesis is a statement about what the researcher feels she/he will find. Inductive research demands the stating in advance of the specific information sought. Anticipating what will be discovered can have its drawbacks, sometimes causing the researcher to make the prophecy come true. It is for this reason that Chicanos are attracted to participant observation. It allows those living the life to render what their own reality is. For example, in the Bessemer study, I simply wanted to know the nature and character of life in the barrio. Drawing upon the suggestion of Alfred Lindsmith (1947), I undertook a good part of the literature review after the data was collected in a deliberate attempt to limit bias in the research. Prior observation of life in Bessemer provided a standard for judging the literature without being under the sway of the literature's influence and enabled me to understand the source of the literature's errors and distortions. This approach diminishes biases by not allowing too many preconceived attitudes about life in Chicano neighborhoods to influence the conclusions. This part of the research is linked to the conceptual framework, the theory that will reveal both similarities and dissimilarities with what is discovered in the literature review.

The Chicano scholar's choices have consequences that are both negative and positive. In making a professional choice to conduct Chicano research and to disseminate her/his findings, the scholar joins a social trend that hopes to produce a population that is sensitive to science and the Chicano condition. The scholar also seeks to strengthen that trend so that the existence of Chicanos with a healthy lifestyle becomes a social reality. This inheritance includes nudging, and sometimes shoving, the country into learning to live with and to respect Chicanos and other Latinos. This is the ideal. The demand on Chicana/Chicano professors by academia, by Chicano students, and by the Chicano community is extraordinary, and this can be difficult on the Chicana/Chicano professor. In addition to their personal needs they have the career demands of gaining promotion and tenure, as well as requests for assistance from a large community with many needs and celebrations of its own. For many Chicano scholars a career in Chicano Studies becomes a lifestyle. This lifestyle often is imposed upon them by liberal members of the dominant society and other non-Chicano entities seeking assistance, guest lectures, consultations, and other services. In summary, the Chicana/Chicano activist scholar is a very busy person. The successes, graduations, and celebrations are positive contributions because they tie the Chicano academics to the larger community, and they are then not isolated in their jobs. There is continuity. The Chicano academic immediately contributes toward making the world a better place to live in; but this can be a stressful undertaking.

For the widest and most updated source of research on Chicanos the student is referred to unpublished master's theses, doctoral dissertations, and journal articles found at most university libraries. Not only are there few Chicano articles published in comparison to non-Chicano articles, but until recently they have been difficult to attain. This search for the latest publications is now facilitated by computer technology and interlibrary loans. Any good piece of academic research must include not only a literature review but must also detail the methodology used to obtain data.

SELECTING A RESEARCH TOPIC AND A METHODOLOGY

A general literature review may reveal an area in which the student wants to concentrate, but so do the student's personal interests, based on a variety of experiences or hobbies. Selecting a topic includes library research with a focus on secondary as well as primary research that is either qualitative or quantitative, or both. The collection of original data is part of primary research, while the reorganization or evaluation of data collected by someone else is secondary research. Methodology involves how to conduct the research after a topic is chosen. The student must decide what factors will be measured and what sampling technique will be used. Methodologies may be experimental, surveys, or participant observations. In experimental designs the scholar is interested in manipulating variables, characteristics that change, in order to establish the cause and effect of relationships. In a survey a number of people are asked the same set of questions. In participant observation subjects are watched. In Bessemer, for example, I employed participant observation because little was known about the nature and character of Chicano communities. Chicano Studies were relatively new and I began with a blank slate and a desire to observe what the population did where they lived. Participant observation is recommended to those who like and work well with people and who are interested in the details of how a behavior is arrived at.

When conducting research, a description of the methodology is important because it enables other scholars to know how the study was conducted so they can design similar studies. With this knowledge, a later study on the same community utilizing some of the same approaches may be undertaken. A description of the methodology allows the investigator to measure changes in the community over time (longitudinal studies) and to assess if changes in the methodology are necessary. It assists in the development of methodological approaches by contributing ideas on what works and what does not work when studying a specific community.

The Bessemer study was patterned on the classic traditions of W. Lloyd Warner's *Yankee City* (1963), Elliot Leibow's *Tally's Corner* (1967), William Whyte's *Street Corner Society* (1955), and the Lynds' *Middletown* (1929, 1937); but the primary methodological influence was Herbert J. Gans's *Urban Villagers* (1962). All of these scholars were influenced by the work of Dorothy and W. I.

Thomas, the founders of participant observation as a model. Their work will be more fully discussed in chapter 5. Gans maintains that social scientists must observe people in their normal everyday life to discover their everyday mannerisms. He used participant observation in his study of the west end of Boston because it enabled him to get close to the social realities of life in that neighborhood. I selected participant observation as the method by which to study Bessemer because it allowed me the most freedom in the analysis of a society that was not homogeneous. Only by using a method that allowed me the versatility to delve deeply into a variety of topics could I hope to develop an adequate picture and analysis of the Bessemer population, which would set the groundwork for more specific research.

In the early 1970s, John Lofland (1971) wrote that participant observation refers to the circumstances of being in or around an on-going social setting for the purpose of making a qualitative analysis of the setting. This method is a technique by which the investigator attempts to verify hypotheses through direct observation of the participants. Although I had some idea of what might be encountered in the field, I did not enter the field seeking specific information except in a few areas, like housing. In participant observation the researcher leaves herself/himself open to whatever occurs in the field.

The literature on participant observation becomes somewhat confusing when discussions of the structured, unstructured, direct, and indirect approaches are presented. At one time or another the Bessemer study utilized all of the above mentioned approaches. Perhaps, this was due to the interdisciplinary nature of community study. The interdisciplinary nature of Chicano Studies, its tendency to draw from several academic fields, is also evident in the Bessemer study because communities do not conform to academic limitations. In utilizing several approaches, I found the writings of Dennis Poplin (1972) very helpful. I also followed Gans and utilized six major approaches. Informal visiting and formal interviewing of residents and community officials were two of the techniques I employed. Several of the community members served as respondents to questions that clarified misconceptions, gave additional information, or place phenomena within a social and historical context.

I purposely structured interviews with open-ended questions. I knew what questions would be asked before I conducted an interview. Most frequently one question led to another; just as one community contact led to another. There was only one consistent "informant," a 68-year-old male who introduced me to others and gave me inside information on what was happening and why. The informant usually took the lead in contacting me when he felt something was happening in which I would be interested. I was not consciously seeking out this informant. He was a consequence of my talks with several people, where I let them know what I was doing and that I wanted to talk with others. Actually, the informant emerged somewhat as did those of William Whyte and Herbert Gans, as a lucky coincidence. The conclusions in the study are my own, but the informant was a most helpful person, not only during the data collection phase but also in some of the analysis. In the study, I changed the informant's name to protect him from potential, unintended, consequences of the research.

Whether or not to inform subjects that they are being observed is a matter of personal choice, or ethics, and will be further discussed in chapter 4. The Bessemer informant was a former CF&I steelworker and a one-time disc jockey who was retired and working part time for a community senior citizen's agency. He was born in Mexico and had lived in Bessemer since he was a very young child. Mr. Dominguez rendered information about meetings and the social and political structure of Bessemer. He was most valuable in revealing information about what was not generally known about Bessemer and its people. He and other community members were subject to observation, and most of the subjects directly observed and interviewed were informed that I was conducting research. However, there must have been a few individuals who were observed, from a distance, and were probably not informed of the study. It is impossible to let everyone in a large community know they are being observed. The researcher must also be careful to ensure that the observation does not change the behavior of those being observed. As of this date no one has objected to my study; in fact, people have been very supportive. For added insurance, as in the Bessemer study, it is recommended that the student obtain written permission from subjects. There are situations that are dangerous, where the observer or respondent would be at risk if her/his identity were known. In this case, change the name or identity of the respondent.

SAMPLING

Sampling consists of an orderly selection of representative members of the community. It can consist of representative cases or individuals from the larger community. There are some areas to consider when undertaking sampling. From what population was the sample chosen? Does it represent the entire spectrum, or only persons who are middle income, senior citizens, or mothers with children? How was the sample chosen? For example, was every third person interviewed? The size of the sample is important, too. If it is too small it may not adequately represent the population. Generally, the larger the sample, the more the results can be depended upon.

As has been mentioned, a qualitative study might be criticized because the respondents did not constitute a systematically selected representative sample. In the Bessemer study little effort was made to secure a representative sample in a strict statistical sense. Instead, sampling focused upon age, income, and gender and consisted of those encountered in the field. To this degree, it was random and limited to those encountered. This was done because my research was exploratory. In the tradition of Alfred Lindsmith's *Addiction and Opiates* (1947), the purpose of the study was not to secure a representative sample but to establish a general description of the field and to set the groundwork for the analysis of life in the barrio.

METHODOLOGY AND THE
SOCIAL-HISTORICAL CONTEXT

Generally students should assign names to the different sections of their research. A minimum of one section should be devoted to the social-historical context, the historical evolution of the development of the research topic in the literature review. It is important, when conducting Chicano research, to note the social-historical context in the methodology. The name of the section should reflect what is being focused upon. In books the various aspects of a topic are often identified by subheadings or chapters. Books assist in guiding a student in the use and selection of subheadings. When the focus changes, the subheading should be changed. In the Bessemer study, for example, the literature review chapter was entitled "The Development and Maintenance of a Dual Society." This was done because at the end of the literature review it was clear that two very distinct societies existed side by side, with two very distinct sets of social standards, in this southern Colorado community.

The literature review for this study revealed that models, designs, or plans for studying race relations existed but needed to be expanded to place the community within a social-historical context. Most social scientific analyses include a fundamental, unwritten assumption that populations exist as they were encountered in historical isolation. Without this lead the student might assume that communities simply existed. They were not fashioned by past social experiences. The Chicano Studies model for conducting research in the Chicano community focuses upon the social history of the community, and it deals in depth with the impact of that social history upon contemporary conditions. These conditions, in turn, are shaping the future and in essence are the past of the future.

Looking at this social past is also helpful when studying substance abuse and violence. Chicano scholars have made major delicate decisions on how to document violence linked to racial tension. Communities can no longer ignore this process and the fact that racial relationships have been characterized by conflict, dominance, and subordination. There has always been racial tension, and it has helped shape and maintain contemporary conditions.

The social-historical context will be outlined to help evaluate the student's community with regard to race relations. Some communities may vary substantially because not all are as old as some of those in New Mexico, Texas, Arizona, and California and not all developed in the same direction. Nevertheless, patterns are evident. These patterns reflect the impact of the U.S. war with Mexico (1846), the number of Latino residents, the diversity among them, and how discrimination manifests in the community.

INTERNAL COLONIAL MODEL

Early Chicano social scientists reacted to theoretical models that were in place when they arrived on the academic scene and evaluated them as inappropriate. In response to the dysfunctional, "Chicanos as abnormal," or deviant models there appeared the theory of internal colonialism. This construct has dominated the study of Chicanos for over 20 years. The model was used to analyze the data collected in Bessemer. In 1978 it was useful, but it was not sufficient to explain sexism and outline how to empower the community. The student of the Chicano community should conduct a similar test in order to establish not only the saliency of the model but also to promote new knowledge, new theoretical models.

Internal colonialism will be further discussed in regard to theory, but for now the student should know that it is an extension of Marx's class analysis and his work on capitalistic imperialism (1848) and that she/he needs guidelines when developing a methodology. One such guideline is the focus on internal colonialism. Various elements of race relations theory are incorporated in this model whose appearance in Chicano Studies began with Robert Blauner's internal colonial perspective (1969). Blauner maintains that racial prejudice is largely a product of racial ideologies that were developed to justify structural discrimination. In other words, racist behavior exists because racist thoughts and beliefs are held. These beliefs justify the behaviors that work in society to exclude certain people. Primary examples are found in employment practices. Job competition between Anglos and racial minorities increases racial tension, prejudice, conflict, and violence. One group dominates and controls land, people, and resources. The conquest is complete only when the environment has been polluted and the people are unable to produce and consume any more. Dominant and subordinate populations may intermingle and there may be no geographic entity separating them from one another, but there are distinctive differences in the quality of life. The dominant and subordinate groups must interrelate, although they frequently live in segregated space and the degree of discrimination varies according to social history and population density. How have Chicanos survived such an oppressive experience?

The Chicano community that I studied is what Erving Goffman (1961) called a total institution. From the beginning Bessemer was self-contained. Workers were paid by the steel mill. They bought groceries at the company store and lived in company housing. Their children went to company schools and life could be lived without leaving the area. To an extent Bessemer continues to be self-contained. Most, if not all, that people needed was/is within walking distance. But, Bessemer was also a psychological concept, an idea about space. In the minds of Bessemer residents, and nonresidents, it is still a definite area inhabited by certain kinds of people with distinctive characteristics.

The steel mill has historically influenced the Bessemer community, both environmentally and psychologically. Perhaps the physical, tangible aspects of its heavy influence are most apparent, for it is the largest employer and the largest taxpayer. Along with its growth, there came a number of bars, restaurants, and other small businesses that still characterize the community. Eating, drinking, and dancing are major forms of recreation. As in the early days, housing was mixed and varied in quality in 1979. In 1881, Dr. Corwin, a steel mill employee in charge of the Sociological Department, had built a two-room hospital. Today,

St. Mary Corwin Hospital bears part of his name. It is located in Bessemer just a few blocks from the area where Dr. Corwin had his last facility. The mill continues to color the air, and the ditch that the CF&I once had a need for still runs through the community. People have buried those who have drowned in it, and the memory of lost loved ones lingers. Those with flooded basements and rats in the summer are continuously reminded of the ditch. Only a few remember that the mill was instrumental in having the ditch built. The physical influence of the mill is obvious, but its psychological and social influences are subtle. The CF&I continuously used class, race, and gender as a means of dividing its working-class population, thus keeping them from organizing and striking.

The attempt to place the community within a social-historical context is a Chicano Studies methodological approach. It very quickly revealed, in the Bessemer study, that southern Pueblo (including Bessemer), Colorado, was once part of Mexico, and that it was, and still is, heavily populated by Spanish-speaking people. The first settlers in Pueblo were Mexicans. Teresita Sandoval, her parents, and her Mexican children were the first residents of Fort El Pueblo long before the arrival of any railroads and steel mills. This history was missing from regional history books.

THE AMERICANIZATION PROCESS

Early attempts by the CF&I to "Americanize" its workers were racist and generally disrespectful of the workers' culture. At the time they were considered good industrial sociology and psychology. Corwin's contention that ethnic boys would grow up to be mill workers and the girls would become wives of steel workers was both racist and sexist. His programs were purposefully manipulative of the working class. In essence, the Sociological Department brainwashed women into female gender roles, using them to pressure men into male gender roles, and to work harder at the mill. At no time does H. Lee Scamehorn (1966) show that CF&I officials encouraged ethnic males and females to leave the mill to seek higher education or to become doctors, lawyers, corporation owners, or other professionals. Instead, the attitude of mill executives cemented into the minds of the early Bessemer population the roles of working-class men and women.

The beginnings of a community cannot always be identified with precision. It is not always easy to establish when Anglo-Chicano relations began and when they became antagonistic. Anglo contact with the Spanish in Colorado, for example, began with Zebulon Pike and the conflict over his trespassing. In Texas relationships were at first relatively peaceful, but turned sour after the Anglos would not obey Mexican law. What is certain, though, is that conflict continued. In Texas the conflict resulted in the U.S. war with Mexico and the conquest of the Southwest by the Americans. From 1870 to 1874, Felipe Baca, Colorado territorial legislator, actively opposed Colorado statehood because it would allow the northern territory, heavily Anglo populated, to dominate the southern territory where Hispanos had controlled the land for generations. New Mexico also resisted statehood. Anglo-Chicano conflict is still evidenced in the language used by both groups to describe the other. In 1979 Anglos referred to Chicanos as "greasers" and "taco benders" and Chicanos called Anglos "gringos" or "honkys."

With this conflict in mind, the researchers must be vigilant and well informed before entering the field. They should have some idea how community members relate to those who are not members of their community or ethnic or racial group. If this information is not available or if the objective of the research is to document this relationship, caution and sensitivity are advised. With long-term, bilingual, U.S. born Chicanos, the cultural differences between the two groups and the researcher (if the researcher is of a different culture) appear to be few, but they do exist. Unfortunately, in today's society cultural and racial conflict is on the rise. Some communities have dealt with it very well, others are hostile to one another, and violence has occurred.

REFERENCES

Blauner, Robert. 1969. "Internal Colonialism and Ghetto Revolt." *Social Problems*, 16 (Spring): 393–408.

Camarillo, Alberto. 1979. *Chicanos in a Changing Society*. Cambridge: Harvard University Press.

Cohen, R. 1979. *Culture, Disease and Stress among Latino Immigrants*. Washington, D.C.: Smithsonian Institution.

Frammolino, Ralph. 1993. *Los Angeles Times*, November 20, p. 11.

Gans, Herbert J. 1962. *The Urban Villagers*. New York: Free Press.

Goffman, Erving. 1961. *Asylums*. Chicago: Aldine Publishing Company.

Grebler, L., Joan Moore, and Ralph Guzman. 1970. *The Mexican American People*. New York: Free Press.

Leibow, Elliot. 1967. *Tally's Corner: A Study of Negro Streetcorner Men*. Boston: Little, Brown and Company.

Lindsmith, Alfred. 1947. *Addiction and Opiates*. Chicago: Aldine Publishing Co.

Lofland, John. 1971. *Analyzing Social Settings: A Guide to Qualitative Observation and Analysis*. Belmont: Wadsworth Publishing Company.

Lynd, Robert S., and Helen M. Lynd. 1929. *Middletown: A Study of Contemporary American Culture*. New York: Harcourt, Brace.

————. 1937. *Middletown in Transition: A Study in Cultural Conflicts*. New York: Harcourt, Brace.

Mannino, F. V., and M. F. Shore. 1976. "Perceptions of Social Support by Spanish-speaking Youth with Implications for Program Development." *Journal of School Health*, pp. 13, 46, 171–74.

Marin, Gerardo, and Barbara VanOss Marin. 1991. *Research with Hispanic Populations*. Newbury Park: Sage Publications, p. 14.

Marin, G., and H. C. Triandes. 1985. "Allocentrism as an Important Characteristic of the Behavior of Latin Americans and Hispanics." In R. Dian-Guerrero, ed., *Cross-cultural and National Studies in Social Psychology*. Amsterdam: Elsevier Science Publishers, pp. 85–104.

Marx, Karl, and Friedrich Engels. 1964. *Communist Manifesto*. In Arthur Mendel, ed., *Essential Works of Marxism*, pp. 13–44. New York: Bantam Books. Originally published in 1848.

Moore, Joan W., et al. 1979. *Homeboys: Gangs, Drugs and Prison in the Barrios of Los Angeles*. Philadelphia: Temple University Press, 1979.

Munoz, Carlos J. 1972. *The Politics of Urban Protest: A Model of Political Analysis*. Claremont, Calif.: Claremont Graduate School of Government.

Poplin, Dennis E. 1972. *Communities: A Survey of Theories and Methods of Research*. New York: Macmillan Publishing Co., Inc.

Scamehorn, H. Lee. 1966. *Pioneer Steelmakers in the West*. Boulder, Colo.: Pruett Publishing Company.

Trotter, Robert, and Juan Antonio Chevira. 1981. *Curanderismo: Mexican American Health and Religion*. Athens: University of Georgia Press, 1981.

Valle, R., and C. Martinez. 1980. "Natural Networks among Mexicano Elderly in the United States: Implications for Mental Health." In M. R. Miranda and R. A. Ruiz, eds., *Chicano Aging and Mental Health*. Washington, D.C.: Government Printing Office.

Warner, W. Lloyd. 1941. *Yankee City*. New Haven: Yale University Press.

Whyte, William Foote. 1955. *Street Corner Society*. Chicago: University of Chicago Press.

Elderly woman surrounded by memorabilia, 1994.

4   Entering the Field and Gathering Data

Herbert Gans (1962) understood the complexities of deciding which approach to take when entering the field. This chapter discusses these complexities and guides the researcher in conducting field studies on Latinos. It notes that Gans did not extend a perspective on the significance of gender, and advances that gender is of significance when entering the field. This chapter will elaborate upon my experience as a female researcher and as a Chicana feminist scholar. This chapter continues the discussion of whether the researcher should inform subjects that they are being studied. It guides the student through the data-gathering phase, with emphasis upon how collecting and organizing the data in preparation for data analysis has been assisted by computers and the Chicano Studies perspective. A most important element of this chapter is how to treat a non-finding as a finding.

ETHICAL CONSIDERATIONS

Gans maintains that if a researcher hides the purpose of the study, then it is done because there is no other alternative. If the scholar bares all her/his research purposes, she/he may be denied access to the very society that is to be studied. If the scholar gathers data solely by interviewing, she/he can only get reports of behavior, not behavior itself. If the researcher is completely open about the study, respondents may hide information or they may exhibit the appearances of a behavior—not what people really do, but how they would like their doings to appear in public.

In the study of Bessemer, I chose to be a known observer. I took caution not to oversympathize with the community because I was Mexican American and shared ethnicity with those being observed. I had full confidence in my ability to enter into community life, study it, and detach myself enough to analyze it. I also chose to inform my respondents because I knew that gender can define what kind of sources are available to the female researcher. I hoped that the cloak of research would legitimize my activities to those who may have had gender biases. After entering the field, I came to distrust this assumption. But introducing myself as a researcher did give me much more legitimacy in the rather compact community than I would have had as a Mexican American woman or as a Chicana feminist who was simply going around asking questions.

I chose to inform my respondents because I did not want to hide all my note talking. While living on the street in the early 1970s and studying Anglo street people in Boulder (1977), my notes had been burned. They were frequently stolen even though most of the respondents knew I was doing research. Maybe that occasion had called for more anonymity, but I did not feel it was necessary in Bessemer. In the final presentation of the data, I changed most of the respondent's names, but not the names of organizations or their locations because one objective of the study was to provide the community with a document that the citizens could use. At the time of my arrival in Bessemer, the community was encountering great difficulty in being recognized by local non-Latino, elected officials and health providers. Basically, the Chicano-controlled health centers were taking business away from private doctors. I was seeking to fulfill the objective of Chicano Studies—to do applied research that would empower the community. This approach is linked to the cultural idea of reciprocity, which will be introduced later in the text.

ENTERING THE FIELD

When entering the Chicano/Latino community, the researcher needs to be culturally literate. This usually means being adequately prepared to speak the verbal language and understand nonverbal cues, and being knowledgeable in the cultural traditions of use of language, body language, greetings, and conduct with various age groups and genders. In addition, the length of time for observation should be decided upon before entering the field.

I observed the Bessemer Chicano community for 15 months. The observation period was strongly defined by the fact that I had lived in the city of Pueblo, on the far southeastern edge of Bessemer, while doing my undergraduate work (1970–1972) at the University of Southern Colorado. This experience and some knowledge of the area and its people facilitated the 1978–1979 study. I entered the field slowly. In 1978 I spent four days—Friday, Saturday, Sunday, and Monday—every two weeks for nine months observing the community. In early spring of 1979, my family and I moved to Pueblo from Boulder and rented a home on the south central edge of Bessemer. While living in the area, I continued the observation until very late in the fall, when I had enough material to begin the analysis phase.

Entering the field begins the data collection phase, which entails a systematic way of gathering information. I began walking up and down streets, trying not to be too obvious while taking notes on what I saw. I sat in the park, watched, and talked to people. To learn more about the area, I turned to the telephone book and city directory and studied them intently for ethnic names, the nature of businesses, and the map that would later be used to establish the community's boundaries. From the "city government" listings I got some names of persons and called for appointments with city officials. I talked with individuals from the Human Resource Commission, Social Services, the city's Transportation Department, the Police Department, the Health Department, and the Pueblo Regional Library, where I did most of the literature review on Bessemer. I frequented businesses and got to know people by making it a point to talk to them each time I saw them. For example, on my early morning walks I noticed the same woman working in her yard. One day I briefly talked with the woman about her flowers. Four days later I saw her outdoors cutting her lawn. I stopped to discuss her yard and flowers in more depth and told her what I was doing. I called on her from time to time to walk through the yard and to get to know her, her family, and her neighbors. Once in awhile my research was the focus of our conversations.

In entering the field and conducting a community study, the participant observer will encounter some difficulties. Bessemer, was, and still is, a relatively safe place but some communities are not as peaceful. Students conducting research where there are gangs, gang warfare, drugs, mentally ill street people, and risky situations such as gun sales and protests should exercise extreme caution and should know everything possible about the community before entering it. Some pertinent information includes population characteristics by race, income, gender, and sexual orientation, as well as crime statistics, the police, community maps, and possibly an informant or contact in the community. In high risk communities it is recommended that the researcher should not make her/his initial entrance into the field alone or enter without anyone knowing she/he is in the field.

It might be difficult to duplicate a participant observation study, like Bessemer, because of the human nature of the individual researcher, the changing social and human circumstances, and geographic region. Each investigator varies in personality, training, social/cultural skills, and experiences. Also, communities are not stagnant. In every population there are economic and social fluctuations, political factions, cliques, and quarrels. Although the researcher may have a problem in maintaining neutrality, she/he must always strive toward it. To maintain neutrality the researcher should develop personal and social conflict management skills and know that the research has priority over personal opinion.

While studying Bessemer I contacted roughly 175 individuals. On several occasions I had opportunities to observe large groups of people by attending public festivities: for instance, the Colorado State Fair Fiesta Day Parade attracted thousands. In this line, I attended the Colorado State Fair; Saint Francis and

Our Lady of Assumption church festivals; public meetings on city pollution, health, mental health, community development funds; and numerous political fund-raisers.

The investigator has the advantage of not being institutionalized in the setting that is being studied. Because the researcher is not firmly engrossed in the norms and assumptions of the community, neutrality can be retained by making the study and community the focus of her/his loyalties. Latino communities are highly political places. Community residents, politicians, and organizational members will confide in and attempt to bias the researcher. The student is advised to listen and try to extract from the confidants an explanation of what is happening and why it is happening. When analyzing data, the researcher should step outside of what was reported and draw upon research skills to make conclusions. This is sometimes very difficult and the researcher may feel like a "spy," even a "sellout." The most important things to remember are the objective and priorities of the study.

SELF-EVALUATION UPON ENTERING THE FIELD

Because most Chicano/Latino researchers have been trained in Eurocentric institutions, it is possible to repeat the mistakes of non-Chicano/Latino investigators and come up with cultural bias. In essence, one becomes what one is taught. As has been mentioned, the participant observer working in the Chicano community should be concerned with respect and reciprocity, which is a form of implied reciprocacy, return, repayment, or exchange. The recompense is frequently in the familiar form of exchange of services and material goods, but deep down it is much more than that. It is about repaying, or being paid for, a visit with a visit, a smile with a smile, a dirty look with a dirty look. I reciprocated to the community for their participation, their cooperation, in the study in several ways. I exchanged flower seeds with the woman who worked in her yard. I sat on the board of the Community Youth Organization, attended the South Side Health Center emergency meetings, donated to political fund-raisers (regardless of party) by purchasing raffle tickets, cookies, cakes and candies. I frequently visited those who befriended me. Some relationships become life-long commitments, but the student should be careful not to be too available in order not to lose perspective. For example, when people discovered that I was "educated" and that I knew which herbs would soothe common ailments, I often gave counsel on personal and professional problems or prescribed herbal treatment. I also began to act as a referral service to those less informed about their community. But, this began to take up too much time, and I had to monitor my time. The most important thing the researcher can do is produce a study that is holistic, but well balanced.

In my experience, people, especially racial, ethnic people, want to be written about. If treated in a nonthreatening, supportive, and interested manner that is characterized by respect and a personal approach, people will cooperate and tell the researcher just about anything. Social activist scholars and younger scholars are highly energetic and attracted to participant observation for this reason. Perhaps this is because it is in their interest to observe their community. The young and the activist scholar may have more energy for the intensity of the work, but they may also have another reason. Younger scholars have a tendency to like and want change. They are hopeful and interested in the quality of life in ways that have not been tarnished or quieted by experience. Nevertheless, the benefit of experience is just what the older scholar has to offer the younger academician.

VERSATILITY AND THE COMMUNITY OBSERVER

There were many things for which I was not prepared when conducting research in Bessemer. I was prepared to be treated as an outsider, but I was not prepared to be as obvious as I was. I had come to the area from Boulder, a predominantly Anglo university town, with a middle- and upper-middle-class population that had many elite tendencies. Bessemer, in contrast, is an area of poor and working-class people of color. I was familiar with the area. I was also Chicano and knew about poor and working-class attitudes and values because they reflected my background. I forgot, however, that at least in appearance I did not look and act like the people of Bessemer. I had acquired a Boulder style. I entered the field with my inherited light olive complexion and auburn hair in an Afro American permanent curl. Like other Bessemer youth, I wore jeans everywhere I went. This was unlike Bessemer women who, at the time, had one dress style in private and another in public. Women my age tended to "dress up" in polyester trousers when they went to the bank or to visit the priest in the rectory. Very few women, even the young ones, went without a bra. When I first entered the field I did not wear a bra, but I soon learned that it was distractive. In Boulder, normal street attire consisted of tweed blazers and jeans. My tailored gray, wool blazer, hiking boots, and blue jeans seemed to be drawing attention, but not as much as my gray sweat pants stuffed into gaucho boots and topped with a t-shirt covered with an open flannel shirt. I changed the blazer and the sweat pants for a darker-colored sweater and some polyester trousers when I was told that I looked "funny."

Not many women past the age of 13 rode ten-speed bicycles; I did. This was unconventional, but not deviant. It was also convenient and an inexpensive form of transportation. I kept this practice up because it was a versatile means of transportation. On the bicycle I could stop between buildings, ride down the alleys, and cut across parking lots. I never had to pay parking fees, but I was frequently worried about having to lock the bicycle up.

In several ways my age was an asset. I was not too old to talk with the youth nor too young to relate well with the elders. Other pluses were my bilingual and bicultural ability. Although the principal language in Bessemer is English, most senior citizens and many youth are bilingual. With recent Mexican immigrants, Spanish was mandatory. Anglos only spoke English. With seniors, I tried to see which language was preferred. It usually was Spanish. Senior citizens were happy to speak Spanish with someone much younger. Speaking Spanish with the non-English speaking residents opened doors that might have been otherwise closed. I also had good street sense. Having a teenager in my home kept me current in popular American music and general youth culture.

A question arises: Because of the negative relations between members of the dominant class and those of Chicano communities, does the researcher conducting research in Chicano/Latino communities have to be Chicano? In 1979 the answer was yes. Today, despite various types of methodology, the answer is "it helps." Participant observation is difficult when the researcher has to cross class barriers (Gans, 1962), but it is much more difficult when race and/or ethnic barriers must be overcome. Until discrimination no longer manifests against Chicanos/Latinos, social scientists doing field research can benefit from the insurance that being Chicano/Latino offers. This does not mean, however, that Anglo scholars should keep away from conducting research in communities of color, it only means they must guard against their cultural biases. They should study American race and ethnic relations extensively. Courses in Chicano Studies are required, and the non-Chicano researcher must be fully aware that even though she/he may not intentionally mean to offend, their very presence sometimes offends those who have felt the pain and misery of historical traumatization.

Chicanos need to be academically prepared but they also need to bring to the field a full understanding of personal and internalized negativity that may trigger certain reactions. Without this understanding the Chicano academic may also bias the findings. Surely, knowing the Spanish language and having a Hispano appearance and a Chicano nonverbal behavior are positive attributes. Sharing some underlying assumptions about how to eat, talk, stand, walk into a church, and greet an older person is a plus. Familiarity with the geographical area and knowing the spiritual nature of people are other pluses, as is skin color because Latinos can be dark complected, although not all have dark features. Last name is a great identifier, but raza also have non-Latino names.

Most U.S. born raza have been educated in a Eurocentric middle-class tradition. Eurocentric, middle-class Anglos have conducted most of the research. For a long period of time this research has been held up as a superb example of how to do research. Even though some of this research has been severely criticized by indigenous populations, it is cemented in academia. One example is the study on gender roles conducted by anthropologist Margaret Mead (1970) in New Guinea. Another is a study of curanderismo in San Antonio by psychiatrist Aria Kiev (1968). Finally, there are many works criticized by Octavio Romano in "The Anthropology and Sociology of the Mexican Americans" (1968), which has been reviewed in chapter 2. Thus, the researcher should also possess class and cultural fluidity and should be able to deal effectively with homophobia as well as sexism and racism. The researcher cannot assume whom the respondent will identify with. In Bessemer, I interacted with African Americans, Italians, and Serbians of various age and income levels. I entered working-class bars and dirty vacant lots to talk with "winos." In my Boulder street study, gender became a factor when I was threatened with rape by a much larger male, simply because he took a dislike to me. Gender was a factor when I teamed up with a teenaged female who delivered a baby while living on the street. In my experience, being a woman can be a positive or a negative depending upon the situation and the environment. Living on the street is not safe for females. There are situations that are fairly gender neutral, like reading in the library, but gender always plays a role. The researcher is advised to be flexible in the field, to not depend upon gender, and to develop gender fluidity as a tool by which to gather data. Gender fluidity means role norms are to be used selectively and with self-respect. There are times when the gentleness of females is appropriate, and there are times when very assertive behavior is mandatory. Because Bessemer was so highly impacted by the steel mill and the huge male workforce, I was very much aware that I was a female cast in a female role. People were generally surprised by, but highly interested in, what I was doing. On a few occasions I was teased. One day I walked into a barbershop and told the owner, who was cutting a young man's hair, who I was and what I was doing. I had forgotten my gender role, as he informed me he did not think he had anything important to say about the nature of doing business in Bessemer. The man in the barber chair started laughing, as did the barber and the two men waiting for a haircut. One of the men waiting exclaimed, "A chick writing a book!" They all laughed out loud. I now recognize that at the time, 1978, a barbershop was considered a male space.

OBSERVING BOUNDARIES AND TAKING NOTES

The researcher should proceed with the assumption that the community is the residents' space, not the researcher's. Thus, boundaries must be observed. This is especially important when researching indigenous communities and elements of the sacred. City government officials in Pueblo, Colorado, had little or no social criteria for determining the physical or social boundaries of Bessemer. While I have discussed outlining the physical boundaries, the researcher must outline the community's description of its living space. This may differ from the official outline. The researcher must also outline her/his own ethical, physical, and social boundaries in order to prepare for times when community people violate them. This violation may or may not be intentional.

To determine the physical boundaries simply ask people who live there. To establish how big the community is in terms of physical and social space, I would recommend that the researcher begin with the number of people. When doing this, keep in mind that there are many people who have not been included in official counts. Physical landmarks are important because people give directions and define where they live according to them. These landmarks are symbols with special meaning. Physical landmarks might include ditches, bakeries, hospitals, factories, murals, churches, grocery and drug stores, parks, bridges, water towers, or streets. When encountering minor disagreements about where communities begin and end, the researcher may clarify the boundary by asking if a landmark is considered within or outside of the community. After this is done, the student should draw a map of the community. City, state, and federal maps can be utilized for this purpose but keep in mind that much more than physical space is being analyzed. Color coding may be helpful. Find out what people think and feel about areas within their community.

Data is generally collected in the form of notes that are taken, rewritten, edited, indexed, filed, and refiled. These notes are later used to construct a narrative. In Bessemer, I would walk or ride my bicycle from one end of the community to the other taking a different direction everyday. On a few occasions I drove my car around the boundary, parked, and walked to the central business area. At first I took notes on everything: the time, weather, conditions of the streets, who was out, what they were doing, what they were saying, and with whom they were talking. I counted houses on blocks, what was in trash cans, and what happened in the alleys, vacant lots, and buildings. As the study progressed and I felt I had enough information on the physical description of the area, I concentrated upon the people.

A good researcher does not leave home without note-taking material. She/he never knows when someone or something will appear that might add to the study. Researchers have been known to write on napkins, matchbook covers, scrap pieces of paper, even on their hand. Always note the date, time, and place. Sometimes notes are in terrible condition because they have been taken under pressure or have been forgotten in pockets and subjected to laundry. I first took notes in a very small spiral-bound notebook. The notebook was easy to carry but did not allow enough writing surface. The small pages were difficult to file and difficult to read. I developed the tendency to write smaller than usual, but it was uncomfortable so I changed from the small notebook to a yellow, legal-sized tablet and then to sheets of note paper that could be easily manipulated. I made a clean copy of the notes after leaving the field. Rewriting notes makes them legible and stimulates thinking.

During my 1978–1979 study, people did not have home computers. Computers not only facilitate keeping notes clean and organized, but second copies can be filed, cross-referenced, and indexed much more quickly and thoroughly. In the Bessemer study, I kept two files: a chronological file and a subject file. During interviews I used a portable tape recorder. Today, smaller, hand-held recorders are available. At the time this was much more expensive. Batteries quickly ran low. An extra set of batteries is a necessity. The objective is to be as inconspicuous as possible. When taking notes, allow ample writing time. Allow for a right- or left-hand margin large enough for indexing at a later stage in the project. Hand-written notes should be read, corrected, and rewritten as soon as possible because detail escapes the memory. Numerous software programs exist that can assist with indexing, but if the student is a visual learner she/he might begin by filing all field notes in one manila folder. This file will soon become so bulky that other files will need to be added. Label each file clearly with the subject headings of what you have observed: BUSINESSES, EDUCATION, CASE STUDIES, HEALTH, HISTORY, COMMUNITY ORGANIZATIONS, HOUSING, CRIME/POLICE, LEISURE TIME, ADOLESCENTS, DEATH AND DYING/RELIGION, MEDIA, EMPLOYMENT, POLITICS. Files on the different phases of the study are also important: ENTERING THE FIELD, PHYSICAL DESCRIPTION, DATA COLLECTION, ANALYSIS. Not only do they assist in writing the methodology section of the report, thesis, or dissertation, they may help document new aspects of methodology. Alphabetize the files and do not integrate them into a general filing system. If working on a computer, create a directory and file everything regarding the project within it. If working manually, create a special file cabinet for your project. As the study continues more subject headings may occur, so may ideas that explain what is happening in the community. Save these explanations in a file marked theory or conclusions. Keep in mind that a non-finding is a finding. When something that is expected is not found, the student frequently ignores it. This may be a major oversight. What is not discovered may be very important and very interesting.

DATA ANALYSIS

Once the data has been collected, the scholar must begin making sense of it. There are two aspects to this phase, the physical and the intellectual, and they are connected. This phase demands both physical and intellectual manipulation of the data. Through the data analysis, hypotheses can be supported or not supported, and conclusions can be reached. From conclusions will come generalizations about the community. It is in this phase that concepts are defined and theoretical statements are produced. These statements explain the relationships and interrelationships between behavior and other aspects of the community and why they exist. A key to this process is questioning the researcher's assumptions.

Indexing is part of the data analysis process. The analysis cannot be made unless the data that has been collected is organized, and this is where indexing enters the picture. It can begin when it is noted that certain themes or subjects keep emerging. Many times these appearances are not expected and the study becomes as exciting and challenging as not finding something that was expected. Data collection has changed with more dependence being placed upon miniature, voice-activated tape recorders and computers.

The following example outlines indexing. It represents the material filed in the physical description file. Note that the time and date are referenced. The note begins with housing and is indexed accordingly on the left-hand side of the paper. It documents conditions of yards and the nature of the weather on April 24th, 1979, at 2:00 P.M. The last entry mentions Mrs. Archuleta, who became one of my informants, and references what she was doing outside of her home. This note became important when comparing female to male work. When the physical description chapter was completed, the remaining notes were filed under "sex roles." Academic language has changed in the mid 1990s, and a more politically correct title for the file would be "gender roles." Indexes can now be generated on a computer on separate pages with a few relatively simple strokes of the keyboard. Computers also assist with cross-referencing of files and directories. In 1979, I did cross-referencing by hand utilizing smaller pieces of paper that were pink, instead of the yellow notebook paper that the notes were written upon.

Sample of Indexing

Apr. 24, 1979	I noticed today: Closer to the
housing	business district there are more
	houses on each block (12–16). Further
	from the district there are fewer homes
	on each block (8–11). The ones further
front yard	from the district are in better condition.
	The ones closer in, worse. Most of them
back yard	had lawns in front but none in back. The
	ones further from the district tended to
	have more back yard lawns than did those
spring weather	closer in. It was cool today in the morning
	but the afternoon warmed up by 2:00.
women's work	Mrs. Archuleta was hanging clothes . . .

Writing up the notes and the results can be relatively easy. It is important to write at a time that is consistent with one's own body rhythm. Some researchers write best at night; others write best very early in the morning. Writing does not come easily to some. The key is to be consistent. Work on one chapter at a time. Do not try to write a masterpiece the first time around. Writing requires reworking the data and sometimes rewriting several times. If a block is encountered, proceed to the next section or the next chapter.

Those doing research in the Chicano community contribute greatly when they identify concepts and offer their perspectives on what is taking place. These perspectives can become theories, and theories can revolutionize how researchers conceive and behave toward the community. These changes in conceptualization and behavior are frequently discussed in regard to paradigm shift, the broadest and most consensual way of thinking about and doing things. For example, the concept of *verguenza*, shared or communal shame, has contributed much to the area of mental health. What was considered shyness, lack of motivation, laziness, factors explaining why there was a lack of individualism, became more clear when Chicano scholars documented and defined verguenza.

Every body of knowledge has its founders or persons who have revolutionized the field. Sociology, for example, has Karl Marx, Max Weber, and Émile Durkheim as some early important figures. Basically, what these men are credited with is lending direction to the leading assumptions in their field of study.

They did this within the tradition of academics in the university setting and at professional meetings among colleagues, who reviewed, accepted, rejected, or adapted their perspectives. Chicano students, researchers, academics, philosophers, and social activists have produced Chicano Studies, which has similar founders and producers of knowledge and basic assumptions. The oldest university in our hemisphere, for example, is located in Mexico. Chicano Studies has some of its roots in Spain, where Jewish traditions contributed heavily. It has an even more ancient tradition of indigenous ways of producing and distributing knowledge both orally and in writing. It is also, more recently, rooted in the Chicano movement and student activism of the 1960s (Padilla, 1985, 1987). However, in many ways Chicano Studies is not similar to the traditional paths of putting forth knowledge, getting it legitimized and dispensed. Latino academia has networks in various countries and foundations among the grass-root populace of the United States. Sufficient credit has not been given to those who published first, but instead to the many women and men who made it possible for early scholars to enter the university in the first place.

The analysis phase requires that the researcher call upon training and experience; but sometimes the researcher will have to study new areas or revisit material in order to come to a grounded understanding of what has been encountered in the field. Generally it is a matter of extra reading on a subject. While doing the analysis of Bessemer, I concentrated upon congruencies and incongruencies, and I very often found that what people said and what they did were not the same. I reviewed one of my research manuals and discovered attitudinal and behavioral measures. In subsequent studies I was careful to include ways of measuring not only attitude but actual behavior in order to test the saliency of what I reported. In other words, including these two measures allows the scientist to conclude how strong a factor is—for example, to make sure that when people said they believed in something, like going to church, that their belief was strong enough to go beyond verbalization into practice. On another occasion, a verbal interview with an educational representative revealed information that was contrary to what he reported to city officials in the form of statistics. This made the analysis very difficult, and some ethical suspicions of the person who was interviewed surfaced. He and other reporting sources contradicted what community members were saying and feeling. In the writing stage, I solved the problem by reporting the inconsistencies and by treating the phenomenon as sociological findings. In short, a non-finding was a finding.

REFERENCES

Blea, Irene I. 1977. "Street People: A Study of Boulder's Leftover Hippies." Unpublished paper, Boulder County Community Relations Office, Boulder, Colorado.

Gans, Herbert J. 1962. *The Urban Villagers*. New York: Free Press.

Kiev, Aria. 1968. *Curanderismo, Mexican American Folk Psychiatry*. New York: Free Press.

Mead, Margaret. 1935. *Sex and Temperament in Three Primitive Societies*. New York: William Morrow.

Padilla, Raymond V. 1985. *Chicano Studies at the University of California at Berkeley: En Buscs del Campus y la Communidad*. Ph.D. diss., School of Education, University of California, Berkeley, 1974.

———. 1987. "Chicano Studies Revisited: Still in Search of the Campus and the Community." In Alfredo Gonzalez and David Sandoval, comps., *A Symposium of Chicano Studies: Proceeding of the National Association for Chicano Studies Southern California FOCO*. Los Angeles: California State University, pp. 13–38.

Romano, Octavio. 1968. "The Anthropology and Sociology of the Mexican Americans: The Distortion of Mexican-American History." *El Grito* (Fall).

5   Analyzing and Creating Social Space

This chapter reviews the Chicano Studies insider/outsider approach in order to introduce the daily social and physical environments of Latinos. It incorporates the observations that most things make sense and that the analysis of Chicano communities has progressed as Chicano Studies has evolved. This evolution can be studied as interdisciplinary and applied social science tactics, and not only explains how to enter where Chicanos live, but also links the study of Latinos to problems encountered when studying U.S. society, as a whole. This goal leads to a discussion of the social reality faced by Latinas and integrates a feminist perspective within the context of a male-dominated and Eurocentric academy. The chapter focuses upon the contribution of Mexican American scholars to a paradigm shift within the academy and how this affects the mental and physical construction of reality. The chapter explores how Chicanos define themselves by analyzing their own physical and social settings, the theory of internal colonization, and how Chicanos responded to the concept of decolonization. The chapter exposes the melting pot theory, and draws from my own experiences in the development of Chicano Studies and my sociologist training to exemplify how the student can come to conclusions about her/his own research after collecting data. I do this in an effort to guide the student into an area that is not traditionally taught by mainstream public education: critical thinking. Critical thinking has to do with the battle of ideas—questioning and constructing ideas. The chapter shows that there has been a struggle to change old ideas.

SELF-CONCEPTUALIZATION

One of the goals of the Chicano movement was to elevate the self-concepts of Chicanos by allowing the raza to define themselves. Self-conceptualization had

Some Chicano communities are characterized by a high number of bars, and other small businesses not owned by community members. These establishments sometimes exploit response to racism and sexism.

to do with evaluating how Chicanos were perceived and comparing and contrasting this to how Chicanos saw themselves. This was not done by committee. This was a process where not everyone and every group developed at the same time. In fact, some communities experienced a sort of cultural lag while others developed quite rapidly toward gaining a critical consciousness. To understand this, an interdisciplinary approach was necessary.

The interdisciplinary approach was rooted in Chicano Studies. Because Chicano Studies is a young field, it is still growing and changing. To foster, direct, and monitor this process the National Association of Chicano Studies (NACS) was founded in 1972, with the purpose of promoting research that would empower the community. This association sought to correct and advance the obscured and distorted depictions of raza in academia and in U.S. society by challenging the structures and mechanisms that did not allow Chicanos equal participation and representation. The founders of NACS sought effective solutions that were not detached from the historical development of the Chicano experience. At the time of the conceptualization of NACS, political activism, social change for Chicanos, was based upon research, and change was, indeed, the goal. NACS has not deviated from that initial role.

NACS documents discrimination and creative energy in the barrio and offers not only healing but also culturally salient avenues for expression of the contemporary condition and its development. NACS strives to remain true to this role by allowing community members and academics to join it. Its members construct theories that explain the basic dynamics of the Chicano interaction with Anglos, with Mexico, and among themselves. NACS also promotes social predictions and identifies indicators of the future. Sociologists in NACS have supported Chicano Studies, drawing from the foundations of sociology, where Weber contended that in order to understand the behavior of groups of people, it was necessary to understand the meanings the individuals attributed to specific behavior. Weber's emphasis was upon understanding how people understood what was happening (Marindale, 1968). In the Chicano movement this is presented as a grass-roots perspective.

Of equal importance is value, worth that is attached to behavior. In essence, social behavior is given social meaning by those closest to it, and that meaning is defined by cultural norms that sanction or unsanction behavior. Chicanos and Anglos frequently disagree on these sanctions. It is for this reason that Chicanos demand that they be given opportunities to put forth their perspectives. Simply, Weber believed behavior should be studied within its own cultural context. Weber (1958) rejected Marx's idea that economics determined all social relationships and maintained that religion was at the base of capitalism. Although I reject both perspectives and postulate that there is an interrelationship between a variety of social variables (religion, economics, politics, the criminal justice system, education), it is useful to look at what Weber had to say. His writings will help the beginning researcher understand what prompted Chicano academics to continue their work.

Weber added a dimension beyond religion to social science. As was mentioned earlier, this is an area in which there is much controversy. Weber (1970b) argued that sociology should be concerned with establishing what is a "social fact"—with uncovering the patterns that exist—not with making conclusions about what ought to be and what is not. This, of course, frustrated Chicano academicians, and they simply tossed away his notion because they were very well aware of the politics of science and the social fact that discrimination existed. In the nonviolent tradition of Mahatma Gandhi and Martin Luther King, Jr., they resisted.

TOWARD AN APPLIED SOCIAL SCIENCE

Chicano social scientists, like some social scientists before them, were concerned with what to do with the knowledge they gained from studying social patterns. It was the end of the industrial period in the United States, and some of their people were dying and subjected to physical and emotional mutilation in jobs that exploited them. These jobs paid so little money that Chicanos could not house, feed, and clothe themselves. They could not gain medical attention and quality education that would support the pursuit of knowledge. Education, up to that time, and even now, is primarily an Americanization process. The researcher should note that Chicano social scientists did not slip into judgmental postures; they had lived this reality, and they were seeing it continue. Because of the differential between the workers and the owners of the means of production, the work of Karl Marx attracted some. Others resisted Marxism because it relegated all workers to the working class and did not allow for the dimensions of race. The following paragraphs provide the student with a quick overview of the leading trends of thought that influenced Chicano academics after they discovered Marxism and the work of Émile Durkheim. Some of these theories share underlying assumptions. These assumptions have influenced the study of U.S. race relations, but they do not fully explain the Chicano experience. There are two schools of thought into which many of these studies fall: (1) the structural functional school, more typically characterized by the work of Herbert Spencer and Émile Durkheim; and (2) the conflict school of thought characterized by the work of Karl Marx. Out of these schools of thought, Chicanos have identified the following major categories of theoretical frameworks.

The *Race Cycle framework* postulates that ethnic and racial minorities come into contact with the dominant culture, compete for resources, are accommodated by the social system, and assimilate into the system (Glazer, 1975; 1974; 1971a; Glazer and Moynihan, 1963). This model does not take into consideration the viciousness of the system of prejudice and discrimination and how it deters accommodation because it is unwilling to accept cultural differences.

The *Consensus framework* maintains that the social values of racial or ethnic minorities will converge with dominant values over time and assimilation will eventually take place (Parsons, 1951). This model also does not take into consideration the viciousness of a system that entraps certain people into positions of powerlessness, that deters assimilation by imposing phenomenal costs, nor does it consider that those in power do not want to abnegate that power.

The *Interdependence theorists* contend that ethnic groups will interact and cooperate regardless of unshared values in order to make social gains (Durkheim, 1964). This model assumes people are traders. They will trade their cultural identity because they need certain things. It renders a depiction of racial and ethnic groups as willing to give up salient survival mechanisms in order to get a piece of the American pie. Conquered people do not do this easily.

The *Conflict model* views conflict and coercion as central features of structural adaptation and necessities of change (Dahrendorf, 1959; Coser, 1959). This model is oppressive. It beats the racial or ethnic community into going along with the social plan or endure the consequence of nonconformity. In this model conflict will evolve to produce a call for revolution and the overthrow of the oppression of the capitalist system, resulting in the emergence of a classless society. This contention offers a radical resolution. The eradication of the oppressive system and the emergence of a society without divisions may have been attractive to the disenfranchised of the 1960s, but it was never very practical because the disenfranchised did not control resources. Conflict theorists do not see the world as consensual or stable. Competition is a key factor. It causes pressure upon the system because of conflicting relationships that result from competition. These theorists see the world in terms of struggle and conflict with the need for radical, more urgent, change. Tension and conflict are the source of change, and change can be violent. The model's focus is upon understanding the process by which people win and lose in a hierarchical structured society, and it concludes that the process is structured to benefit those with the most resources.

Structural-functional theorists assume that there are components to the structure of society and that each component of that structure has a function, a role. If each part of society plays its role, society continues with stability, harmony, and little or very slow change. Gradual change occurs through adaption to new social needs. Outmoded structures are eliminated. When the components work together, the entire society benefits. In their models social patterns contribute to the maintenance of the society, and society is stable. Chicano Studies scholars have criticized these models but draw from them to identify the emergence of social structures, the roles of social components, and the forces within them that oppress Latinos.

The above-mentioned contentions are opinions. Some of them are based on research, but they, basically, are ideas that developed on university campuses where traditional ways of thinking have been preserved. Marx, Weber, and Durkheim were Europeans who very strongly influenced American social science, which was also strongly influenced by social Darwinism. Social Darwinism is the application of the evolutionary theory of animals to human social behavior

(Leyburn, 1968). Chicanos inherited these traditions when they appeared on campus and quickly learned how they had impacted the structure of the general society.

Unlike traditional social sciences, Chicano Studies had its beginnings in the civil rights movement, in Chicano communities, and off campus. Chicano Studies was more holistic than traditional social science in that it concentrated on skin color and, eventually, gender; but it also sought to address the issues of low employment, low educational attainment, lack of political representation, low health level, and high incarceration rates. This meant drawing from more than one academic tradition. At the time, young men of color were disproportionately dying in Vietnam. All the issues of the time were brought onto campus by individuals who are now middle-aged and older. Chicano Studies contends that to promote critical thinking, students need to know the whole picture. They need to know how universities and ideas, or knowledge, evolve. They want to know how students of color came to have the opportunity to obtain higher education and what the structure and function of that education meant to them. Just as communities need to be studied within social-historical and cultural contexts, the student is educated within social-historical and cultural contexts. This means that students have been taught in traditional ways because it has served the needs of society to Americanize future workers and consumers who stimulate the labor market. Basically, this outlook supports the status quo.

EUROCENTRICITY AND MALE DOMINANCE

The reality is, however, that citizens must be world centered, but because of traditional U.S. ideas, the dominant members of this country are ill equipped to meet world demands. The United States has encouraged knowing one language and one culture. The country's obsession with European Anglo culture and its English language now places it at a severe disadvantage in world relations. For a long time the United States has had economic power, and it has used this power to control; but it has also practiced racism, which has lost the country credibility because it validates the "ugly American" image. Eurocentrism has been practiced in international politics, and it has been promoted by social scientists. Many cultural groups have tired of this approach.

The idea of Eurocentricity was cemented in sociology when sociologists studied northern and southern European immigrants in the early part of the 20th century. As mentioned in chapter 2, these social scientists were concentrated at the University of Chicago and contributed greatly not only to the development of community studies but also to another area of concentration, social problems. Because U.S. racial and ethnic groups did not comfortably fit into Eurocentric analysis, they were viewed as problematic. This left Chicano Studies with the legacy of analyzing Latinos as social problems and as immigrants. Chicano Studies, of course, does not accept the social problem categorization of ethnic/racial citizens and does not believe the immigrant model applies to Chicanos. It reminds academicians that Chicano indigenous ancestors were not immigrants and that the first European immigrant populations were their Spanish ancestors. In fact, Chicano Studies teaches U.S. history from south to north and includes white East Coast settlement patterns which extend west, as part of the conquest of Indians and Spanish colonialists. The westward movement takes place after the country was thriving as a result of Spanish settlement patterns that began in the southern part of the hemisphere.

Chicano Studies is more supportive of the social scientists who developed a kind of sociology that stressed the meaning of social behavior and promoted social action. These scholars sought to understand society, but they also wanted to do something about it. Dorothy and W. I. Thomas (1928) emerged with a situation argument that could be used to analyze Chicano communities within the social context. The Thomases argued that individuals attached their own meaning to situations. These meanings are subjective because they have important consequences. If people define a situation as real, then the belief is real and has real consequences. W. I. Thomas was among the first to graduate from the University of Chicago sociology program. He conducted research among immigrant Polish groups and had a fundamental disdain of Herbert Spencer's evolutionary (social Darwinism) thought. Chicano Studies shares this disdain. Thomas developed a research methodology that provided systematic ways of uncovering the subjective meanings of behavior. This methodology will be focused upon in the last chapter and is called participant observation.

Aspects of analytical models often overlap. This is how knowledge progresses. In sociology, for example, Chicanos have also drawn from symbolic interactionism and role theory to explain their research findings. Symbolic interaction maintains that society is made possible by the development of shared meanings for symbols. This perspective confronts the subjective, cultural meanings of behavior and the process through which people develop and communicate shared meanings. Chicanos share some of the dominant society's meanings for certain symbols (this makes them bicultural), but there are other, more subtle consequences to these symbolic meanings due to Latinos' low social position. In addition, raza also have symbols that are not part of the dominant structure. It is the task of the Chicano researcher to identify, document, and extend these meanings in order to strengthen the culture of U.S. society.

Role theory emphasizes that people play a role in society just as they do in a scripted play. Erving Goffman (1961) analyzes social situations in terms of the roles people are cast into. Those who control have written scripts for the less powerful, but the players take advantage of opportunities for improvisation. Improvisation is individual, but it can be group action, and it can change the content of the script. Role theorists are attentive to the patterns of interaction, standard parts in the social theater.

Chicanos do not want to play the role they have had in U.S. society for over 200 years. In fact, they do not like the play and stay away from theaters. Chicano

Studies maintains that race, class, and gender cannot be delineated utilizing traditional theories. These theories are grounded in experiences outside the Chicano experience. This is why the internal colonial model is so highly favored. It is not only rooted in the Chicano experience, it calls for decolonization. It does not, however, outline the process of decolonization. The element of decolonization, doing away with oppressive forces, requires that the process of internal colonialism be dissected. This can be done by analyzing Anglo culture, how the English language is structured, and how this structure affects its culture. Anglo culture and the English language are hierarchical, they place high or low value on objects, creatures, and human beings. Anglos are considered "good." Latinos and Latino culture have been looked down upon. This value structure has endured because Anglo control the forces that legitimize.

One of the forces that legitimizes is education. In education, the melting pot theory was dominant until the early 1990s. The internal colonial model was a direct response to the melting pot theory, which assumes that minority assimilation will take place and that it will be evidenced by intermarriage, the sharing of customs, attitudes, and various skills. Assimilation may be rapid, as was that of European immigrants; or it may be much slower, as has been the case with African Americans. Examples are given of European immigrants who experienced disadvantaged social conditions but who, through hard work and the adoption of dominant ways, made social gains. It is posited that if Chicanos follow the examples of the European immigrants, they will also experience social gains. The question remains, "Why has this not happened?" It has not happened because Chicanos are unwilling participants in the dominant society. After their conquest in 1848, their rights were violated, and they continue to be violated to this day. Conquered people do not give up their culture as easily as do volunteer immigrants. The consequence of this resistance is poverty.

In keeping with the assimilation-accommodation model is the notion of a "culture of poverty," which was developed in the 1960s during the War on Poverty. Some social scientists assume that to understand the writings of anthropologist Oscar Lewis (1966, 1965, 1960, 1959), who extended the culture of poverty is to understand the American Latino, Puerto Rican, Mexican, and Mexican American family. This misplaced assumption basically contends that the poor share universal values, beliefs, and attitudes about life. The poor possess a distinct subculture that does not allow them to share in the dominant culture typified by middle-class Americans. The poor are presented as pathological—incomplete versions of major elements of the middle class, fatalistic, and self-generating in that socialization mechanisms perpetuate the cultural patterns that make it impossible to escape from poverty. This assimilation-accommodation model cites a lack of education and the failure to organize politically as the major drawbacks of the poor. It is maintained that through participation in acceptable and established institutions, such as education and the two-party political system, the poor will experience upward mobility. Chicanos have participated, and they have experienced discrimination.

DESCRIBING THE FIELD

Contemporary Chicanos need to know a minimum of two cultures in order to function as well-balanced human beings in society. Thus, the researcher needs to know these two cultures. In most cases Chicanos know more about American Anglo culture than Anglos know about Chicano culture. A testimonial to this contention is the reality of the Bessemer experience. It had/has much in common with other Chicano communities. It was/is, however, also very different because of regional economic and political influences and because of its isolation from the Mexican border. Chicano Studies outlines both the differences and the attributes shared with Anglo culture in order to help the student understand cultural relativity (the patterns that endure), the need for decolonization, and the daily lives of Chicanos.

For example, Bessemer is in Pueblo, Colorado, a community characterized by its hot summers and cold, sometimes relatively mild, winters. It has a working-class character. At the time of the study, the major employer was the Colorado Fuel and Iron Corporation. It is still the major employer. The original study differed from other studies in that it concentrated upon Chicanos as working-class, not highly impoverished, individuals. It also analyzed the everyday life of Chicanos as they balanced class discrimination, racism, and sexism. Thus, the study documented the community as a creative, not a passive, entity.

Bessemer had a small business center where several physical features stood out. The most outstanding feature was Bessemer Park. Here, youth gathered to socialize, engage in courtship, and sometimes argue with one another. Families picnicked or played in the park on Sundays and on weekdays children could take swimming lessons. Some, especially senior men and teenagers, visited the park every day. This same situation can be seen today in most urban communities; but where Bessemer had its share of neighborhood winos, in some areas there are street people and drug dealers who also use the park. Because the study took place in southern Colorado, where the winters are harsh, the weather had an influence on how much time people spent in the park. In winter residents sought refuge indoors but were seen crisscrossing the park, using it as a shortcut between destinations. Bessemer winos were different from large city winos (in fact, this term is rarely used). They were long-time residents of the immediate area. Some families were selective about when they visited the park. Some would not let their children go to it without supervision. Other children ran through it freely, unsupervised. Then there were those who visited primarily in summer when there were many softball games.

There was a privately owned ice cream stand in the park. From 11:00 A.M. to 11:00 P.M. (both in winter and in summer), people of all ages, incomes, and ethnic backgrounds could, and can, be seen purchasing cold drinks, potato chips, sandwiches, candy, and ice cream. People of the area were friendly and talked very casually. On one winter visit to the park, two older men thought I was "from the city," a city employee. They insisted on showing me the park and the stagnant pools of water, graffiti, and broken water fountains. They were hoping I could do something about fixing them. Except for the owner of the ice cream stand, who was Anglo, the park population consisted of many Chicanos, fewer African Americans, and hardly any Anglos. In the summer the lawn was green, and the baseball field was well kept. There were no flowers except around the modern swimming pool, where there were also the only bushes in the park. The park was one square city block in size and was well shaded by large, broad-leafed trees. The first summer of my observation revealed some Sunday afternoon entertainment in the park in the form of Chicano music.

Over the years, this has been replaced by watching football on television. When television football games moved to Monday nights, women engaged in more visiting and shopping. On Saturday nights couples went dancing to live band music.

People used cross-streets and businesses as landmarks in order to give directions and to outline boundaries. To the north was busy Northern Avenue, upon which was located a Texaco station, a Safeway grocery store, and the Yellow Front-Checker Auto store until the early 1980s. A computer software firm has since moved into this location. Housing conditions appeared crowded, with an average of ten homes on each block. Traffic continuously flowed up and down Orman Avenue on the west end of the barrio; but to the south and east, Central Avenue and Pine Street were relatively quiet. During the fall and winter, there was very little vehicle or pedestrian traffic on these streets. In the summer the pace quickened with people going and coming all day long. There were no Spanish-named streets in Bessemer, unlike other cities with large Chicano/Hispano populations.

The Bessemer Park was not the only park in the area. At the southernmost boundary was the Far South Park. This was a newly created park consisting of recently transplanted, evenly spaced trees. Neither this park nor the Bessemer Park had a facility that could be used to check out recreational equipment—baseballs, softballs, basketballs, bats, canoes, tents, shuffle board sticks, and pucks. Although residents wanted a swimming pool at Far South Park, there was not one at the time I lived there and there still is not one.

Generally I found four factors that fashioned how leisure time was spent: money, social contacts, fads, and traditions. Money, of course, was a primary factor. Those who had none, or very little, "hung around" together. Hanging around has been discussed in many studies of urban youth. Sociologist Gerald D. Suttles (1968) includes such a discussion in his Chicago study of African Americans, Italians, Puerto Ricans, and Mexicans. Those who did have money often spent their leisure time working on hobbies, rebuilding automobiles for men, gardening for women, and other interests like biking (motorcycling). With money they had transportation out of the barrio, and they went on vacation (generally to visit relatives), hunting, fishing, camping, or drinking in bars.

In the late 1970s the people of Bessemer concerned themselves with health, religion, education, and politics. They played, rested, and worked hard at things that reaped no economic return but produced great community loyalty. "Low riding" was rapidly becoming a popular leisure activity in Bessemer, and this trend continued until the late 1980s. Low riding has its roots in Chicano urban barrios. To be a low rider, in Bessemer, was to spend leisure time and money on repairing, remodeling, and custom decorating late model automobiles.

The low rider gave way to the "cholo." A cholo was a youth with deep urban roots in the "zoot suiters" and the *pachuco* activities of the 1940s and 1950s. Young adults rode in cars around town, "cruising." On summer Sunday afternoons they cruised around the city trying to pick up "girls." The girls were actually young women, and some were referred to as cholas. They, like the cholos, had a particular style of dress. They frequently accompanied their boyfriends and complained that cars and other male friends were more important to them than they were. The automobile held a prominent place in this culture. The most outstanding features of the automobile were the paint job, the interior, and the "lifts." Lifts were hydraulic jacks installed to raise and lower the car. Car hopping was a contest where automobile owners challenged one another to see who could make their car jump the highest using the hydraulic jacks. The person whose car bounced the highest won the contest. This was an expensive hobby and most low riders worked, some at the steel mill. Not all low riders adopted the cholo dress and lifestyle and not all cholos were low riders, but automobiles played an important role for both.

Family and house parties have always taken place in Chicano communities, but due to the high cost of nightclub entertainment and the depressed economy, in the late 1980s house parties became even more common among the youth. Nightclubs were still places of much socializing in 1980, but by the early 1990s Chicano youth tended to congregate at home and in the streets. By 1994, drive-by shootings were severely disrupting previous cultural inclinations to socialize on the front porch or let children play in the streets, like they did in the early 1970s. Weddings were still a popular form of family entertainment but, in the 1990s, guests were asked to bring their invitations in order to prove they had been invited. Even the wedding music had changed by the 1990s. It became difficult to afford live bands. The wedding band was frequently replaced by the disc jockey who played both mainstream and Mexican music.

Younger boys in Bessemer and other communities who are not old enough to own a car fixed up bicycles. In the larger communities some of them are in pee wee gangs and engage in illegal activity. The young girls and boys who do well in school are protected by their parents, who take great precautions not to let them get involved in unsupervised activities. Children of working-class parents in Bessemer who could afford the $3.50 entrance fee plus a dollar for refreshments often went to the movies or the skating rink about four miles away. Urban youth who go to movies are attracted to the heroes and heroines of the cinema. Like Anglo parents, Chicano parents worry about the amount of violence at the movies.

In the late 1970s most young men and women wore loose-fitting jeans, t-shirts, and brand name tennis shoes. Both males and females had long hair. In the 1990s the male hair style was much shorter, and shaved heads were evident. Some of middle-class America had moved away from tight-fitting jeans, and all young women and men continued to spend a great deal of time and money on hair products.

In the 1970s, softball was a primary leisure activity. All ages and both sexes played on teams and in numerous tournaments. In the winter there were boxing and pool tournaments. Women were very active in 1970s softball in Bessemer. The Colorado State Hospital and several businesses had, for a long time, sponsored girls' and women's softball teams that participated in organized girls' and women's leagues. The evening games were a welcome break from the intense high arid desert heat. The women were good players and by no means the fumbling "klutzes" of the field that women are stereotyped to be. They played fast and hard, and they played to win. The spectators included men, as well as women and children. The rooting and cheering was just as loud as, if not louder than, that for the men. The city government still supported softball activities in Bessemer in the 1990s, and the teams had sponsors who furnished uniforms, but rarely gave money for travel and accommodations for out-of-town games. In fact, out-of-town games were much fewer in number.

As the years progressed, problems changed. By the late 1980s problems of alcoholism had been complicated by the use of drugs, and the community was no stranger to early death. In the 1990s Chicanos had a disproportionate rate of AIDS.

Women displayed an abundance of social and linguistic skills as they engaged in their *platicas*, their talks, in the 1970s. They frequently assisted one another with ideas and found solutions for problems with children, clothing, makeup, and homemaking. This trend among women continued into the 1990s, but more women worked outside the home and the platicas were much fewer and shorter. Generally, women visit relatives, some neighbors and a few friends. In an overwhelming number of Bessemer cases, women of the 1970s claimed that their best friend was their mother, sister, or cousin. In the 1990s young Chicanas had more friends and acquaintances outside the family. Men had fewer friends and generally socialized with fewer acquaintances, most of whom were co-workers. In the late 1970s, both males and females tended to make their close friends in childhood. In the 1990s this was changing, especially for younger people who often did not have long-term relationships or very close ties to other families.

Some first-hand case studies provide interesting insight into Chicano life. In 1978, I first met Mrs. Chavez, a full-time homemaker whose house was immaculate, not only inside but outside. In 1994, Mr. Chavez is still proud of Mrs. Chavez and maintains she has a "good eye" for interior decorating and landscaping. These characteristics were, and still are, shared by her married daughters, Betty and Helen, who worked outside the home in 1978. Neither daughter kept her home as clean as Mrs. Chavez—either in the 1970s and in the 1990s. This bothers Mrs. Chavez. When she visited "the girls" in the late 1970s she often assisted them by washing dishes or doing a load of laundry. Even today she has a tendency to want to "help" her daughters. When the home is clean, or when "the girls" do not want her to clean, they sit and talk, switching from Spanish to English. Mother and daughters work and talk extensively at the same time. In the 1970s they did liquid embroidery; in the 80s they used thread; but by the 1990s they no longer engaged in this activity. Mrs. Chavez and "the girls" still went shopping, but the daughters could rarely go together with their mother. They worked longer hours. One had gotten a university degree and was more estranged from her mother than the other. Mrs. Chavez was lonely. She and the oldest daughter still planted flowers, but not as many, and they stopped planting gardens in the spring.

The Chavezes also had three sons. All of the sons visited at least once a week in the 1970s. By the 1990s the youngest son was dead, and Mrs. Chavez visited his three children at least once a week. The older son had moved, but the middle son visited four or five times a week. In the 1970s and in the 1990s there seemed to be few secrets in the family. Everyone knew everyone's salary, their joys, and most of their fears. However, the oldest son withheld the problems he and his wife were having with their children. They were embarrassed to be having them. The Chavez family considered itself tightly knit, but they spent less time together than in the 1970s. They gave fewer birthday gifts and fewer presents at Christmas. Unlike other families, the senior Chavezes never did go to bars; even though their children did. They all enjoyed dancing in the 1970s but by the 1990s this activity had stopped. None of the children appeared to be having trouble with alcohol, and there was no indication of drug abuse in either the late 1970s or the 1990s.

The family knew the Ramirezes who owned a bar. The Ramirezes later sold their bar and moved to Las Vegas, Nevada; but in 1978, they introduced me to Clarence. At that time Clarence felt that sometimes families got "in the way of (everyday) things." Thirty-six-year-old Clarence thought he was an alcoholic, but he did not care. He revealed that bars had been part of his life since early childhood. He had shined shoes in the bars and had been drinking steadily since he was 15 years old. Clarence lived in Bessemer until the mid-1980s when he moved to Denver in search of a job. He was 26, had been married six years, and was getting divorced. He moved into a new home away from Bessemer after his divorce, but drove his car through Bessemer every day and stopped in at either the Buffalo Tavern or at the Klamm Shell. He was disabled and had remarried by the late 1980s. In early 1990 he stopped drinking due to bad health.

Conversations in the bar, in 1978, varied from family problems to personal finances, politics, casual references to sex, neighborhood affairs, and religion. In the early 1990s some of the talk was about large city violence, more sex, and the content of T.V. talk shows. In the late 1970s a University of Southern Colorado professor, Jim Halverson, did a study of the bars in Pueblo, Colorado. The respondents in Halverson's study (1978) visited the bars one to three times a week in the afternoons and evenings. He found that bar patrons tended to live on social security or monthly pension checks. Most did not belong to any organizations, and they nursed a single bottle of beer for a long period of time. Halverson documented that the bars in Pueblo were ethnically mixed, but in Bessemer the patrons were predominantly Mexican or Chicano. This make-up has not changed over the years. Generally in the 1970s as in the 1990s, the neighborhood bars were old and dark and smelled of stale beer. Most of the patrons were men, among them several older men who had retired from the steel mill. The bar was a primary point of social contact for many Bessemer residents, including children who accompanied adults.

DECOLONIZATION

Making generalizations or drawing conclusion from research is the final step in presenting research findings. This final step may manifest at professional meetings, on T.V., or in academic journals, magazines, and books. These reports are essential because they enable others to understand social reality and to grow. The research may be accepted as valid, having been well conducted and capable of being duplicated, or it may be rejected because of weaknesses in some aspect of the project: the review of the literature, the definition of the problem, or its methodology, analysis, or theoretical statements. Two of the earliest Chicano Studies generalizations were that there were two standards in dominant society regarding Chicanos, and that there was a very large gap between the ideal and the real objectives and promises of the United States to its citizens.

W. Lloyd Warner and Paul S. Lunt (1942) note that residential arrangements are not haphazard and formless. They have a clear-cut, pervasive order and pattern, and they are sufficiently similar in general characteristics. These characteristics serve to attract individuals similar in status to those already living in the area. These features have helped maintain Bessemer and other Chicano communities as predominantly Chicano, separate from the dominant Anglo population. They are as separate and as unequal as if apartheid were practiced. In fact, Chicanos view this inherent segregation through the internal colonial model. The model contends that Chicanos are a conquered people and that their land is occupied territory. Anglos and Anglo-identified officials carry out deliberate policies to constrain, transfer, or destroy the native population's values, orientations, and way of life. Negative policies and stereotypes are advanced in an attempt to discredit the population and make them feel ashamed of their ways, manners, traditions, values, and language. Anglo-dominated power forces discredit Chicano culture, destroy its leaders, its language, its traditions, and generally impose low self-concepts and low self-esteems upon Chicano people. Because Chicanos are subjected to Anglo cultural values as they are manifested in laws, the economic system, etc., and because failure to conform to policy has severe consequences, especially economic consequences, Chicanos are forced to change their culture, see each other less, and talk less often. This is especially clear in the manner in which the Bessemer Chavez family has changed in order to maintain a reasonable living standard in Bessemer.

Since 1870, "Mexicans" have composed the largest cultural group in Pueblo, Colorado. H. Lee Scamehorn (1966) has documented that "Mexicans" were hired at the inception of the iron works. These mines fed ore to the steel mill. Mexicans were not hired in great numbers for many, many years. Nevertheless, this means that some Bessemer Chicanos have experienced slightly more than five generations of the economic and social influence of the mill. Interviews reveal that discrimination was, and still is, common in the mill and in Bessemer. In 1994, the CF&I could no longer afford to pay its retired workers their pensions. The government had to take over. Did mill owners foresee this? This is a subject for further study, but most of the retired workers were Chicanos. The Anglo conquest of the southwestern Mexicans was political, social, cultural, emotional, spiritual, and economic. It took place over a period of time and an interrelationship among a number of variables can be seen. Negative stereotypes and prejudicial attitudes evolved into discriminatory behaviors that were transferred onto, and by, social institutions in a complex interaction, a network, that makes up the social fabric of the United States. Economic factors may be the most visible, but they are not necessarily the most important. Institutionalized discrimination has taken a toll upon the daily lives of Chicanos—affecting aspects of their lives that sustain them, make them different, and add richness to their life.

Chicanos are entrapped in this system. There are both internal and external factors that keep people from changing their situations, and they do not work in isolation. The interaction between outside forces and inside forces suppress any desire to venture outside of what is known because of possible harsh treatment that may be encountered once outside a prescribed role. This is the function of the colonized mind. Becoming mentally colonized also involves a psychological process built upon physical colonialism and its resulting power differentials. Oppression and degradation are internalized. They become part of the psyche. They leave people unable to bond to the society, to one another. Nor do conquered citizens bond to the educational or political processes, but they can bond to gangs, because solidarity results from gang membership. Unbonded citizens are not mentally ill or in any way pathological. They are reacting in a natural way to anything that is not of their own making or anything that does not value them.

Chicano-Anglo relations did not begin with the U.S. war with Mexico in 1846. In Colorado Chicano-Anglo relations actually started as early as 1806 when Zebulon Pike was captured by the Spanish for trespassing on Spanish territory. In 1819, the Spanish signed a treaty ceding territory to the United States, but it was not until 1846 that U.S. Chicanos became unwilling minorities on their own land.

Internal colonialism has been critiqued by Grebler (1970), and others. These critiques have not taken into account the social-historical context of the development of internal colonialism. Moore, Feagin, and others look down on colonialism and the social condition of Chicanos without seeing their historical development. Chicanos point to the crucial element—the U.S. war with Mexico—to note that colonization, the conquest of people and territory for economic gain, was done within geographical boundaries of the United States and was, therefore, internal. No bodies of water needed to be crossed, but colonialism was still experienced. This is a U.S. legacy. Chicanos had land and labor power that were exploited by the conquerors. Some early Mexicans profited from the exploitation of their own people by aligning with the conqueror, even arranging the marriages of Anglo men to their own daughters. Contrary to common belief, Chicanos do not fall in between the space of assimilation and colonialism. Chicano culture has separate, culturally relevant, social institutions developed or influenced by colonialism, and few people have assimilated. Even though threatened, Chicano culture has not disappeared or been assimilated by choice or to any degree. Much has been destroyed by the dominant Anglo society and the nature of colonialism, but the culture is intact, distinctly mestizo.

Sociologist J. H. Turner (1972) maintains that scholars should focus on the patterns that endured, social institutions, and the intricacies within them. Chicano Studies has done this, but it also notes that there are intricacies among social institutions. Chicano Studies agrees that social institutions are social forces that channel behavior. The institutions define and attribute norms, roles, and hierarchical statuses to people, but there are other links. The linkages are networks, a body of interrelated norms and statuses that are affirming systems to those who can conform. Chicanos cannot conform without too great a sacrifice. Social institutions and norms are culturally relevant, but Chicanos sometimes cannot relate to Anglo norms and values. It is to this perspective that Chicano Studies clings the hardest. Chicano culture is substantially different from the dominant culture. It views its world differently.

REFERENCES

Coser, Lewis A. 1959. *The Function of Social Conflict*. Glencoe, Ill.: The Free Press.
Dahrendorf, Ralf. 1959. *Class and Class Conflict in Industrial Society*. Stanford: Stanford University Press.
Durkheim, Émile. 1964. *The Division of Labor in Society*. Translated by George Simpson. New York: Macmillan and Free Press. Originally published in 1893.
Glazer, Nathan. 1975. *Affirmative Discrimination: Ethnic Inequality and Public Policy*. New York: Basic Books.
————. 1971a. "Blacks and Ethnic Groups: The Difference and the Political Difference It Makes." *Social Problems* (Spring).
————. 1971b. "The Issue of Cultural Pluralism in America Today." In *Pluralism beyond Frontier: Report of the San Francisco Consultation on Ethnicity*, pp. 2–8. San Francisco: American Jewish Committee.
————. 1974a. "Ethnicity and the Schools." *Commentary* 58 (September): 55–59.
————. 1974b. "Why Ethnicity?" *Commentary* 58 (October): 33–39.
Glazer, Nathan, and Daniel P. Moynihan. 1963. *Beyond the Melting Pot: The Negroes, Puerto Ricans, Jews, Italians and Irish of New York City*. Cambridge: The M.I.T. Press.
Goffman, Erving. 1961. *Asylums*. Chicago: Aldine Publishing Company.

Grebler, L., Joan Moore, and Ralph Guzman. 1979. *The Mexican American People*. New York: Free Press.

Halverson, James. 1978. *Bar Room Brethren*. Pueblo: Colorado State Hospital Printshop.

Lewis, Oscar. 1959. *Five Families: Mexican Case Studies in the Culture of Poverty*. New York: Basic Books.

———. 1960. *The Children of Sanchez*. New York: Random House.

———. 1965. *La Vida: A Puerto Rican Family in the Culture of Poverty—San Juan and New York*. New York: Random House.

———. 1966. "The Culture of Poverty." *Scientific American* (October).

Leyburn, James. 1968. "William Graham." In David J. Sills, ed., *International Encyclopedia of the Social Sciences*. Vol. 16, pp. 1–7. New York: Macmillan and Free Press.

Marindale, M. 1968. "Verstehen." In David J. Sills, ed., *International Encyclopedia of the Social Sciences*. Vol. 16, pp. 1–7. New York: Macmillan and Free Press.

Marx, Karl, and Friedrich Engels. 1964. *Communist Manifesto*. In Arthur Mendel, ed., *Essential Works of Marxism*, pp. 13–44. New York: Bantam Books. Originally published in 1848.

Parsons, Talcott. 1951. *The Social System*. Glencoe, Ill.: Free Press.

Scamehorn, H. Lee. 1966. *Pioneer Steelmakers in the West*. Boulder: Pruett Publishing Company.

Suttles, Gerald D. 1968. *The Structure of Sociological Theory*, 3d ed. Hornewood, Ill.: Dorsey Press.

Thomas, W. I., and Dorothy Thomas. 1928. *The Child in America: Behavior Problems and Programs*. New York: Knopf.

Turner, J. H. 1972. *Patterns of Social Organization*. New York: McGraw-Hill.

Volkart, E. H. 1968. "W. I. Thomas." In David J. Sills, ed., *International Encyclopedia of the Social Sciences*. Vol. 16, pp. 1–7. New York: Macmillan and Free Press.

Warner, W. Lloyd, and Paul S. Lunt. 1942. *The Status System of a Modern Community*. New Haven: Yale University Press.

Weber, Max. 1958. *The Protestant Ethic and the Spirit of Capitalism*. New York: Charles Scribner's Sons.

———. 1970a. "Religion." In H. H. Gerth and C. Wright Mills, trans., *From Max Weber: Essays in Sociology*. New York: Oxford University Press. Originally published in 1920.

———. 1970b. "Science as a Vocation." In H. H. Gerth and C. Wright Mills, trans., *From Max Weber: Essays in Sociology*. New York: Oxford University Press. Originally published in 1918.

Women meet in Crystal City, 1977, to address their own issues.

6 Chicana Feminist Studies

This chapter concentrates on the contributions of Chicanas via social activism and academic endeavors. Their work has caused the rethinking of previous approaches to the study of populations, especially populations of women of color and racial/ethnic people. Their involvement links social activism to academic pursuit and goes beyond posing "la Chicana" as a victim of sexism and racism. This chapter highlights la Chicana's coping skills and ability to create under extraordinary adverse conditions. The analysis of la Chicana by Chicanas culminates in a manner that has advanced the social sciences by presenting a holistic, multidimensional interactive perspective that strengthens the Latino community and reestablishes respect for women in that community. The coping skills of contemporary Latinas are placed in a global perspective, extending that many are "international" women and some even have international reputations. The chapter mentions second, and now third, generations of Chicana academics who are teaching, undertaking research, and producing manuscripts that define themselves in a highly technological world.

SHOVING THE PARADIGM

The topic of respect for women is not new in the Chicano community. It is a social, spiritual, physical, and emotional part of the community. Males have always been instructed to respect women, and females have always been taught how to conduct themselves so as to command respect. Nevertheless, internalization of other values has led to mistreatment and prejudice that affect la Chicana's life. In this regard Chicanas are no different from other women. Sometimes abuse lies within their culture but more frequently it is introduced and experienced from outside. Chicanas are subject to several myths and contradictions. One of these contradictions is that, like Chicano males, Chicanas are the physical product of the conqueror and the conquered. This was most evident in how the Spanish males treated indigenous women when they arrived in the Americas. Not only could Spanish men not recognize the role of women in pre-Columbian society, but they sought to destroy much of it to get women to conform to accepted women's roles. To familiarize herself/himself with indigenous roles, the student should visit the anthropological sites in Mexico, and/or read the guide to the National Museum of Anthropology, Mexico City, written by Silvia Gomez Tagle, Adrian Garcia Valdes, and Lourdes Grobet (1985), and read works published in Spanish in Mexico (see, for example, Figueroa Torres, 1975). For interdisciplinary approaches see the work of Martha Cotera (1976), Evangelina Enriquez and Alfredo Mirande (1979), and Irene I. Blea (1988, 1992). Colonialism, Americanization, racism, sexism, and urbanization have taken from the Chicano community the norm of respect once granted to individuals and the special honor once placed on the female gender. Despite this, Chicanas have survived, and this survival is in need of more research. Let there be no mistake: Chicanas are powerful in their families, in folklore, and in spirituality.

An introduction to the formation of Chicana Studies is in order so that the student can use this knowledge to strengthen her/his research. The student should know that there are Chicanas actively working within the social sciences to rid it of gender biases. In order for this to happen in the United States, social science must accept that racial and ethnic people, especially women of color, have something of value to teach and that their scholarship can place American scholarship on the cutting edge of social science. Yet, la Chicana is a stranger in her own field. Other countries recognize that her major work is in delineating the intersection of variables (race, class, and gender.) La Chicana has documented that these variable do not function in isolation, but that they affect one another and can function simultaneously. In order to prove this, la Chicana took her community activism onto the campus and began to define her own history, while paying strict attention to male and Eurocentric prejudice.

The early roles of Chicanas were very different from today's roles. In those roles there were strengths and limitations. The Spanish colonial life of Sor Juana Ines de la Cruz during Mexico's colonial period provides an excellent example. During this period, women were not allowed to receive higher education. Sor Juana entered the convent in order to study. There, her natural intelligence led her to write essays, letters, and an entire theological thesis analyzing the Catholic church and male dominance. Her feminist perspective on men and the church cost her severely. To get her to conform the church hierarchy took her books and scientific equipment from her. Within two years she died. So Juana was the first feminist in the Americas and she has become the cornerstone of Chicana feminism.

After looking at the colonial period in Mexico, Chicanas analyzed that period in the United States, including its folklore, then the Americanization process, union organizing, and the Chicano movement. During the Chicano movement interest turned to *Las Adelitas*, the female soldiers and camp followers of the Mexican Revolution. Biographies of women and much Chicana poetry appeared. This led to novels, journal articles, and textbooks where the intersection of variables was outlined.

To do be able to discuss the intersection of social variables, the levels of various interactions between social facts, and their impact, it is necessary to first examine the existence and function of racism, sexism, and class status in U.S. society. It is also necessary to examine scholarship with a focus on institutionalized inequalities and the political use of research in academia. This political use of knowledge and its dissemination or nondissemination to the community has to do with the control of knowledge and its impact not only upon public policy but also upon the consciousness of the masses and the everyday Chicano quality of life. The activist scholar serves to monitor this control and la Chicana's holistic approach is quite evident in how academic and popular culture have interacted.

FIRST GENERATION FEMINISTS

Chicanas began their class analysis in communities and campuses throughout the country in the 1960s and while working among the poor in the Chicano movement. In the 1960s the number of Chicanos and Latinos in the United States was severely underreported, and few academics predicted that Latinos would have such a large social impact by the mid 1990s. In fact, academics had not predicted the civil rights movement, a rebirth of the women's movement, the hippie movement, and the Vietnam War protests. The word "Latino" was not even used. In the 1960s Americans acted shocked to discover poverty and racism in their country. La Chicana was not. She, generally, was a product of poverty. If she was working class, she still had vivid memories of extreme poverty. When Michael Harrington (1963) opened the discussion of poverty in America in academia, la Chicana was struggling to open the doors of higher education to the Chicano community. Through Lyndon B. Johnson's War on Poverty and the efforts of the civil rights movement, she assisted in making Americans aware of the existence of Chicanos. The country was in a dire state of denial, and the fact that this group existed in a historically downtrodden position was a surprise to most, except, of course, to Chicanos.

Poor people exist in America today in great numbers, and a great number of them are Chicano. Many have little education and minimal jobs with little prestige. Poor Chicanas are often domestics in private homes, janitors in large buildings, and maids in hotels. They are cooks, factory workers, migrant field workers, other seasonal workers, social workers, and therapists. A few are nurses, doctors, attorneys, and professors. Indeed, some are breaking ground into new fields. More often, la Chicana's job is physically demanding, sometimes dead-end, and frequently dangerous to her mental and physical health. There is a high concentration of Chicanas in the service areas, as restaurant and bar waitresses, laundry and garment industry workers, grocery and department store clerks. Frequently they are heads of households and/or may be supplementing another income. Although their work is socially necessary, they are underpaid. They are highly represented among the working poor, and are a testimonial to the fact that the more one works in America, one does not necessarily reap more.

During the civil rights era, Chicanas soon discovered their power. Through life experiences and as welfare mothers, they had learned that the treatment of the poor people of color should serve as a warning to American workers about the consequences of being a person of color. Very early they spoke out about how poor people comprise a cheap labor pool that is always available to those that control the means of producing goods and services for the ruling elite. Chicanas, like their Chicano brothers, became keenly aware that the Chicano poor and working poor are available during times of national crisis, like the war in Vietnam. When regular workers are otherwise occupied in wartime, the social system needs more workers and more soldiers. It generally draws them from the unemployed. In the case of Vietnam, it sent them to the fields of Southeast Asia, where well over 58,000 young men were killed. When the structure needs fewer workers, the poor move into a reserve army of labor to await further employment.

Poverty, however, makes jobs for many middle-class people. In the 1960s Chicanas learned that middle-class Anglos had jobs helping poor people. Social workers, welfare workers, educational and job counselors, food stamp personnel, and medicaid and medicare officers had jobs that were supposed to help poor Chicanos, as did/do teachers, doctors, attorneys, nurses, politicians, and business people. Many employers make money addressing the needs of the poor. The state government is among the highest of such employers. Armed with this knowledge, Chicana academics reached the university and struggled to build Chicana/Chicano studies. There Chicanas have defined their academic role as that of heightening the status of women and documenting the lifework and social-historical contributions of women. The first generation of Chicana academics not only brought attention to the poor, they also highlighted the fact that few Chicanas have become poor—they were born poor and they struggle to escape it.

Like her people, la Chicana was, until very recently, relatively invisible, segregated in ghettos, barrios, and other deteriorating communities. These women were once ignored by political officials and kept out of sight by Chicano culture, Anglos, freeways, factories, railroad yards, industrial plants, laws, and social pressure within and outside of their own community. This has changed somewhat, but Chicanas still struggle to overcome overwhelming odds against patriarchy. While the first generation was paving the way with a feminist orientation, the second generation of Chicanas was in junior high, or middle school. They grew up not having to break through some of these barriers but still advancing the feminist dialogue. Some acknowledge their inheritance and have gone on to produce a third generation of Chicana academics: the urban Chicana. The first generation of women are now highly advanced in education. They are, for the most part, tenured full professors, businesswomen, politicians, and specialists in other fields, for example, Dulce Rodriguez is deputy director for engineering in Dade County, Florida (Julip, 1994).

Those who began the analysis in the 1960s are now 50 to 55 years old. Their review quickly moved beyond class to focus on the study of sexism. The very early position papers, poetry, and research on la Chicana is lost. Women of that era conducted research and wrote speeches that were frequently delivered by men. Even though they did most of the writing, they lacked control over what was written. The publications that were distributed carried the names of men as the authors. La Chicana stayed up all night mixing and cooking the ingredients for the burritos to be sold at movement fund raisers the next day. She knew she was the one who got up early to set up the tables, and she sold the food, generally in the sun, all day long. At the end of the day, the men got the applause and carried the money while she cleaned up and washed the dishes.

She began to say no and to look at her cultural self, her colonial pioneer great, great grandmother, her Mexican *adelita* great grandmother, her *curandera* grandmother, and her mother, her most immediate female role model. She saw strength, but she also saw how she had come to be what she was: disempowered, without land, living in a country controlled by strangers. When this group of brave and very alone women began to center on Chicanas as cultural persons, they began talking to other women about things outside of their relationship with their lovers or husbands. They began to ask, and then to answer, why their situation was the way it was. When they began to research and write, they focused sharply upon their own culture and its men. Culture is the variable influencing their work in folklore, health and healing, marriage, education, mothering, and political activism. As mentioned above, early written feminist statements sometimes carried their names, sometimes they did not. I was surprised when a 21-year-old California Chicana called me in New Mexico to ask if I was the author of a piece of work distributed at a Chicana conference in Colorado sometime during the late 1960s or early 1970s entitled "A Statement on Machismo." The two- or three-page statement had no author attached to it. I recognized the work as mine and asked where she had found it. "In the archives at the Benson Latin American Collection at the University of Texas, Austin," was the answer. I forgot to ask how she found me in New Mexico. At one time I had gone to the archives to do research on some dead people. The young Chicana later came to Albuquerque to interview me. She had a grant, a thing we early feminists did not have access to. Times have changed, but not substantially. The issues on university and college campuses are much the same: access, course content, and graduation.

Chicana focus on culture was pointed out by Maxine Baca-Zinn (1982) when she reviewed three early works: Evangelina Enriquez and Alfredo Mirande's *La Chicana: The Mexican American Woman* (1979), Margarita Melville's *Twice a Minority: Mexican American Women* (1980), and Magdelina Mora and Adelaida

Del Castillo's *Mexican Women in the United States: Struggles Past and Present* (1980). Much energy was expended revising the works of past scholars, and Chicanas also produced classroom textbook material where there traditionally had been none.

The efforts of the first generation of scholars also documented the consequences of deviating from prescribed social roles as the exertion of social control. Sequentially, race (a genetic variable) and/or ethnicity (a cultural and social variable) plus gender (another genetic variable) and class (also a cultural or social variable) interact with one another in complex patterns that render la Chicana severely disadvantaged—or at least perceived to be disadvantaged—in a contemporary stratified society. Since the early 1970s scholars have come to realize that this oppression has rendered some coping mechanisms that need to be identified and tested (Blea, 1992). This takes the scholarship further from the Chicana-as-victim perspective toward the Chicana-as-creative-survivalist perspective.

CHICANA SELF-CONCEPTUALIZATION

Women, especially women of color, have developed a unique way of conceptualizing and coping with life's circumstances, including the existence of Anglo men and women. Chicanas have taken on the responsibly for documenting their story by giving direction to demographic surveys, engaging in vigorous academic pursuits in both quantitative and qualitative analysis, and promoting Chicana feminist theory. Often the way in which these women say and do things is thought of as unusual, strange, or wrong. When Chicanas began doing research, they first reassessed Chicano history. They scoured history books sentences or phrases that referenced them and found the depictions were usually negative. They conducted oral histories and collected stories about their past and how they had been passed on from one generation to another. They wrote about *las Adelitas*, the female soldiers and camp followers of the Mexican Revolution, and they wrote about their personal experiences as well as those of other women. They did not separate their experiences from the experiences of their people. These early Chicana feminists included Anna Nieto Gomez, Ines Talamantez, and Lea Ybarra in California; Martha Cotera, Carmen Tofolla, and Inez Hernandez Tovar in Texas; Rowenea Rivera in New Mexico; and Marcella Lucero Trujillo, Nita Gonzales, and Irene I. Blea in Colorado. These women were joined by many more. They were heavily involved in criticizing higher education and in empowering their communities via the Chicano movement. This involvement influenced their scholarship and led some to create literary as well as academic works.

A prime example of feminist scholarship lies in the work of Marcella Lucero Trujillo, now deceased. Lucero Trujillo was born in Alamosa, Colorado, and died in Denver, where she had been a member of Rodolfo "Corky" Gonzales's Crusade for Justice. While she completed her Ph.D. studies at the University of

Minnesota, she made wonderful contributions to Chicano Studies. Lucero Trujillo was a poet, a writer of short stories, and a researcher of Chicano history. She was a community activist, a feminist, and published in several of the early anthologies that are no longer available. She continuously addressed issues of education, housing, and urban youth. Much of her urban perspective was integrated in the Denver Chicano civil rights movement, where she and many other women, like Precella Salazar and Juanita Dominquez, and many men worked on a variety of Chicano issues in the area of Five Points and the northwest side of town. Her most memorable work told of prison reform, poetry, and the development of Chicano Studies. She combined elements of her analytical and community work in her poetry, and she described the social and physical space around her in an unbreakable relationship. Hers was the first Ph.D. dissertation to analyze Chicana feminist poetry. Lucero Trujillo was among the first to publish feminist poetry. Her unpublished poem (few of her poems have survived into contemporary publication), "No More Cookies, Please," demonstrates how frustrated she was with trying to talk to Anglo feminists about la Chicana at receptions where she was not given the opportunity to speak, but was offered wine and cookies.

Early Chicana feminist poets and academics focused sharply on the social fabric of their communities, where they were and what was happening in them, to render insight into la Chicana's experience with other women and girls. Hernandez's work extended from California to Texas, and, like that of Inez Talamantez, focused upon the indigenous elements in Chicano culture, and how the American Indian and European culture often are the same and yet contradict each other. Especially in the realm of the spiritual, their work is beautiful. These women lived in three cultures.

Early feminist scholarship was consistent with ideological developments in the Chicano movement and the Chicano community. The women named above completed their higher education. They earned master's and doctorate degrees. All of the above-named women eventually taught on university and college campuses, and all advocated Chicana rights. They did this, however, despite much emotional pain and loneliness, encountering much resistance not only from their own men but from other Chicanas and from Anglo feminists. They took the Chicano movement's emphasis on racism and class much further to include sexism. Their holistic approach was undertaken because of the need for money and the opportunities it offered in a capitalistic society such as that of the United States. During the last 30 years, however, the Chicana academic has needed some support from male raza scholars. This has been offered only in scattered bits and pieces. Conditions have changed, however. A few men are now feminists, but still very few discussions focus upon Latinas and their role in the world economy and the world social condition. La Chicana can gain some support for her work here because she has more in common with women of other countries than she does with dominant U.S. women. This reality was/is most evident in the development of the women's movement and Women's Studies.

THE CHICANA FEMINIST MOVEMENT

Feminist interests in the 1960s included female-male relationships, equal pay for equal work, and the right of women to control their own bodies through access to birth control and abortion. Poverty was a white feminist concern but it was nowhere near the top of the list, but for la Chicana it was. All feminists wanted to be represented in higher levels of employment, education, politics, and decision making, but Chicanas also wanted this for their people. Chicano people ranked even lower than Anglo women in all aspects of society.

Chicanas and other minority women struggled to take part in the feminist movement, but the white feminist movement was middle class, Anglo controlled, and more exclusive than inclusive. It was unsuccessful in addressing Chicana and other minority female issues. Women of color, Native Americans, Asians, African Americans, and Latinas, withdrew into their own feminist movements within their own racial or ethnic groups and proceeded with their own brand of feminism.

Chicanas, like black women, never abandoned their men and their communities while striving to gain equal rights for women. Even when they went away to colleges and universities, they tied into their host communities. As black and Chicano women talked and worked with one another, they discovered that they were having the same experiences, both with the Anglo feminist movement and in their own civil rights movements. These "minority" women formed coalitions at white feminist meetings and conferences. They were among the first coalition builders of the American civil rights movement. By forming coalitions they developed an ideology that strengthened the movements, but this ideology has yet to be recognized.

Today, these early Anglo feminist demands seem absurd. They wanted Chicanas to choose between being a feminist and being active in the Chicano movement. Chicana feminists exerted an analysis of the character of the intersection of race/ethnicity, class, and gender. This attempt to educate took place in various communities, at conferences, and on campuses. Neither the Anglo feminist nor the civil rights movements paid much attention. The struggle to get these movements to hear and understand their argument was (to say the least) intense. This inability to listen, to recognize the plight of women of color, contributed to the fragmentation of the U.S. women's movement and stifled its strength and ability to grow.

Until the late 1970s the Anglo-dominated feminist movement remained fragmented on the issues of racism, socialism, class, and sexual orientation. With the exception of racism, both fortunately and unfortunately, much of this has been resolved. When Chicanas were involved with the feminist movement, they tended to sympathize with socialist women who advocated the overthrow of capitalism and the construction of an entirely different social society; but they did not join the Communist or the Socialist Worker party in great numbers. Sexual orientation also became an issue. The word used to refer to homosexual orientation, at the time, was "lesbianism"; and it was far removed from the realities of the predominantly Catholic, heterosexual Chicana. Lesbian Chicanas were seen as a relatively new concern of a very small part of the population in the 1970s and 1980s, but there had always been Chicana lesbians. By the 1990s, Chicana lesbian issues had grown substantially. This is an area in need of further research.

The concern of ethnicity does not become consumed by sexual preference issues. They intersect ethnicity. Homophobia exists among some feminists because heterosexuality has been espoused as the ideal in American society, especially by those of the Christian faith. Homophobic attitudes are similar to those of sexism and racism. Being white Anglo American and male is espoused as the ideal, the beautiful, the fortunate, in society. This sends a viciously twisted message to lesbian and homosexual members of the society, especially to those in the Chicano community, which is highly resistant to homosexual and lesbian women and hardly cares to understand the complexity of the Chicana lesbian reality.

In the social sciences lesbian issues were of some concern to Anglo feminists in the 1970s and 1980s, but Anglo women concentrated their efforts on creating Women's Studies. Chicanos concentrated on creating and sustaining Chicano Studies and there was little discussion between the two disciplines. Neither one made much room for Chicanas as professors and scholars. La Chicana pushed herself onto the scene at this level because she had always been present as an advocate, a student, and sitting on boards of programs. This placed la Chicana in a continuously confrontive role. Each discipline designed a curriculum that centered upon their population's stereotypes, use of language, and perceived social, psychological, and biological differences. Women's Studies analyzed middle-class gender roles, Anglo women and work, women and the law, the history of Anglo women, the capitalistic system, sexual harassment, the struggle for liberation, lesbianism, child care, violence, mother-daughter relationships, friends, and finally third world women. All women of color were lumped together. The tenacious Chicana fit in wherever she could and at the same time developed her own areas of specialization in these fields.

INTERSECTING VARIABLES

It is ironic that at the same time that poor Chicanas were invisible, they also had/have no privacy. Early feminists were forced to secure social services from the government, and were forced to reveal intimate elements of their personal lives to social workers and financial aid counselors. Chicanas found out that the poor are well documented if they seek assistance from their government. This information is, generally, used in budgeting and funding; in national, annual, and biannual reports; and social science research. Further, the police have access to it, and the police are ever present in poor communities, where behavior is constantly monitored.

During the last 30 years of Chicana feminist development, most Americans have blamed the poor, the Chicanas, for their poverty. White Americans often had not experienced poverty themselves, and many still do not recognize the discriminatory tendency to use the poor as examples of what happens to those who do not, or cannot, participate in the norms of society. There are new poor people in the United States, but most mainstream Americans have not witnessed the drastic consequences for those who cannot conform to the norm. The consequences are poverty, homelessness, being signaled out as illegitimate and unworthy, beggars, and criminals. The working class has a slightly different lifestyle, but not very different. La Chicana is disproportionately represented among the overcrowded, living in run-down housing, and characterized by physical exhaustion. For them, like for all poor, the American Dream and all that sustains it promise a better quality of life but do not deliver it. For the working-class Chicana, the major life objective is marriage. Marriage promises independence and the hope for a better life. Educational aspirations, especially a college degree, appear to be on the increase, but the social structure and family pressures may push a young Chicana into early work responsibilities. These pressures, plus any dysfunctional coping skills, may further depress her life chances. While middle-income youth are engaging in sports, hobbies, homework, and dating, Chicano working-class youth are working and/or married. Young men and women are frequently in dead-end jobs, and young women become homemakers and mothers between the ages of 18 and 20. While still young, they are subjected to the stresses of paying bills and raising children. If conditions do get worse, they may include prostitution, drug and alcohol addiction.

Little work has been done on la Chicana as a middle-income person but I would venture to say that la Chicana has weathered the long recession quite well, and a few might have even gained upward mobility. Nevertheless, the middle class generally encompasses white collar workers and other professions. Raza representation may be on the increase, but middle-class Anglos are most frequently used by the media as role model Americans. Chicanos who have successfully climbed into this middle-income group are considered rare and are frequently used as role models for Chicanos in the lower classes. This middle-income group also acts as a buffer between the lower classes and the upper classes, and in fact may not be a class at all in the Anglo sense of value structure. They might just be a middle-income group still retaining Chicano consciousness, or it could be that Chicano consciousness transcends class. This is fertile research territory. The U.S. upper class is very private compared to the middle class, which engages in some conspicuous consumption. It is difficult to say what the Chicana lifestyle is at this level of the class structure. It has been estimated that the Anglo upper class comprises 1 to 3 percent of the population, but that it controls or owns a minimum of 25 percent of the nation's wealth. These figures may be conservative. For the most part, however, these people have inherited their wealth. The wealthy are a tightly knit group consisting of the old rich and the new rich. The old rich have had wealth for generations; the new rich acquired wealth only recently. Although they sometimes cross paths, there generally are few relationships between the two groups. The names of wealthy people appear on the *Social Register*. These people have much leisure time and may discreetly engage in social philanthropy. Chicano membership in this class is rare, but certain individuals, mostly males, in business and the entertainment and athletic fields, have attained high incomes, and can be counted among the new rich.

There was a time when people thought that what we call "sexism" and "racism" today was acceptable. This has changed. Socio-cultural progress began slowly with some feeling that to stop racism was the right and moral thing to do. Today, the argument has changed. Racism needs to be stopped because it is the economic and politically expedient thing to do. Racial and ethnic "minorities" will soon be the majority, and racism costs money. Hispanics are estimated to have at least $98 billion to spend on a variety of commodities, and discrimination is hurting the gross national product and manufacturers.

There is another reason for doing away with sexism and racism: to better U.S. international political power. The world has gotten smaller because of technology. Technology allows Americans to communicate, via a common technological language, with most people around the world. They can travel to the other side of the world in a very few hours. The truth is that most mainstream Americans lack the ability to relate at the international level. In the past, the world was forced to communicate with the United States. Communication, however, is now a multifaceted process, and Americans frequently fall short. Most Americans are monolingual—they speak only one language; and for the most part, they are monocultural—they know how to function in only one culture. This is stressful because it is happening at a time in history when bilingual ability and cultural literacy is an absolute necessity. This lack has cost the United States power, status, and prestige in international affairs.

It is in this arena that Chicanas have the advantage and can teach America, if America wants to learn. It appears that Americans are being forced to learn about balancing more than one language and more than one culture, and are learning how they have mistreated Chicanos for almost three centuries. Chicanos have long reported that their bilingual and bicultural abilities are assets in courtrooms, in business transactions, and in politics. Being able to function in at least two languages and two cultures, however, has not been a valued characteristic in this country, and Chicanos have not been rewarded for their abilities.

CHICANAS IN A GLOBAL SOCIETY

The 1980s examination of la Chicana, during the decade of the Hispanics, was not without its problems. Some of the problems included resistance from a variety of sources, the unavailability of funding, and inconsistent and wrong information. In reaction to this lack of support, Chicanas produced newsletters and monograph series. These publications, however, were produced sporadically and are difficult to locate in university libraries. Many of them were authored by graduate and undergraduate students, with help from their professors. In the 1980s, la Chicana and other women of color were broadly discussed under the liberal label of "third world women." This perspective has been enveloped within the internal colonial model, in part, because the combined Chicana issues of class, race, and gender are rooted in American colonization of Mexico's northern territory. The model is historical; it explains the violence of war, its resulting subjugation, and calls for liberation. These issues are consistent with third world issues that find support in Chicano communities. The issues for la Chicana are much the same as they were several years ago. If there has been any social change, it has been little.

Concentration upon the Chicanas as third world women was based upon the idea that there were two countries controlling the world: the United States and the USSR. These two countries have been referred to as two different worlds. All other countries were the "third world." This ethnocentric view very skillfully places countries that are not the United States or the USSR in a secondary and subordinate position. Feminists adopted the idea of the third world from Anglo, male-dominated language and incorporated it into their language and scholarship to refer to those women who were/are the most disenfranchised from the dominant power structure: black, Hispanic, Asian, and Native American women. It has been forgotten that minority women are also citizens of the United States, and therefore are the political sisters of Anglo feminists.

Chicanas have not criticized the third world perspective. They understand the relationship of the powerful and the powerless in this perspective, but they have not noted that to be called "third world" deprives them of American status. It is suggested that black, Hispanic, Asian, and Native American women be called what they are. To engage in general labeling further alienates American women of color from Anglo women and plays into the male-dominated orientation toward power and the debasement of the powerless. This, plus the early feminist experiences of American women of color, was, and is, an extremely harmful occurrence, one that few women of color forget or forgive. Few Anglo women have even acknowledged this. There has been no apology, no attempt at retribution, and no understanding on behalf of Anglo women that an apology or retribution is even expected. It is, simply, not within their cultural sphere.

Anglo elitism has forced a third world sensitivity on U.S. Latinas to such international issues as the North American Free Trade Agreement (NAFTA) and elections in Mexico. NAFTA's impact on women in this and other countries, the Mayan Chiapas revolt, and the assassination of the PRI candidate for the Mexican presidency are all of primary concern to Latinas who study and/or have relatives, colleagues, and friends in Mexico. The wars in Equador, Guatemala, and other Latin American countries are important to these women, because Spanish-speaking people of color are involved.

SECOND GENERATION FEMINISTS

White women had a history of addressing women's issues in the United States. Chicanas did not. Their feminist history was in Mexico among their indigenous ancestors, the Mexican revolutionaries, in their struggles for liberation against the Spanish, the French, and the upper class. Many Anglo feminists perceived Chicana hesitancy to embrace their movement as based on a lack of feminist experience and commitment. This, of course, was not true. While Chicanas wanted a change in the system, Anglo women only wanted a piece of the on-going structure. In the 1990s, perhaps, this is what most Chicanas want in academia. They compete for very few jobs in academia against Anglo women who have taken Chicana scholarship, reviewed it, and claimed it as an area of expertise.

Most of the leading work on Chicana feminism in the 1970s and 1980s emerged from members of the National Association of Chicano Studies (NACS). I was the first Chicana national chairperson of NACS. Women in this organization produced two major conferences on women and a summary of conference proceedings entitled *Chicana Voices: Intersections of Class, Race, and Gender* (Orozco, 1986). As a result of the work done by women at these conferences, Mujeres Activas En Letras Y Cambio Social (MALCS) was formed. MALCS has produced *Trabajos Monograficos: Studies in Chicana/ Latina Research*, a monograph series featuring the academic and literary work of Chicanas. This work has progressed to the point where well over 100 Chicanas come together to discuss their work and that of other Chicanas at annual retreats.

Hard fought political battles are sometimes forgotten by the younger generation. Some early Chicana feminists have died and some have become less active, while others have become tenured full professors. Community-minded Chicanas and other feminist Latinas have developed unevenly; just as the feminist consciousness has developed unevenly in the Anglo sector of the society. Yet many Chicana feminists energetically continue to pass on the legacy to the fourth generation. They have developed role models in the form of the colonial feminist Sor Juana Ines de la Cruz and Mexican artist Frieda Kahlo; and they have evolved to be role models themselves, knowing that it is necessary to work with each woman where she is in her community, in her own state of feminist consciousness.

Positions of privilege are difficult to give up and many Chicano men still resist feminism, but most Chicano males eventually have to deal with the fact that they need and must value women. Their culture traditionally teaches them this. Somewhere between 1848 and today, some of them forgot it. Chicano male culture has also taught them to respect other people and accept other cultural values. Perhaps this has made Anglo domination easier. Even Chicano and Chicana Studies professors have not totally rejected Anglo-dominated social structure, otherwise they would not be in higher education. Instead, they have very cautiously selected those elements that are not negative. For example, good mental and physical health, although linked to the "gringo" world through the established health care system, are seen as valuable traits for the Chicano. The professionals continue to develop educational policies and programs in the interest of Chicanos. They serve as role models, teaching others to do the same. They have encountered extreme resistance, and some activists view the professionals as "sellouts," or "coconuts," but more and more individuals are recognizing the forces at work and are quick to note what and who works on their behalf and what and who does not. Communities are now more concerned with who protects their interests. This is why they sometimes do not support a Chicano candidate, but the community must guard against stereotyping all Chicanos who run for office. Just because one Chicano was ineffective does not mean different Chicano candidates will not be. Some Chicanos feel that when they get in office they must do what Anglos have done. This does not break the cycle of Chicano oppression, the cycle of internal colonialism.

UPWARD MOBILITY

Discrimination is no longer as profitable as it once was. In fact, it is costing large corporations profit. Chicanas and other Latinas have made great strides in education and in the corporate structure. Unlike education facilities, corporations are not as reluctant to bend the rules. Their goal is to increase profits, even if it means facing a changing market. Their profit margin depends on flexibility. This flexibility has allowed many corporations to move into third world countries to exploit laborers and resources. For this reason most Chicanas are anti–large corporations and often highly critical of Latinas who interact with them.

A special issue of *Vista* (1994) gave insight into Latinas who have achieved some upward mobility in the class structure. As advice to Latinas who desire upward mobility in the corporate structure, Celeste de Armas, vice president of strategic planning for Nestle USA says, "You can't just meet expectations: you have to exceed them" (Roiz, 1994). A positive corporate atmosphere is beyond most individuals' control, and Latinas must be skillful or lucky to choose the right place to apply their energies. There is a select group of Hispanic women serving on the boards of directors and working as corporate officers and high ranking executives. In 1994, Katherine Ortega served on four boards of directors: Diamond Shamrock, Ralston Purina Company, The Kroger Company, and Long Island Lighting Company. Her signature can be seen on U.S. paper money. She suggests that Hispanic women work for companies that provide leadership training, and that they become active in their communities because they need visibility. Vilma Martinez was a member of three corporate boards: Anheuser Busch, Fluor Corporation, and Sanwa Bank of California. She was the first Chicana to serve on the University of California Board of Regents, the first Chicana to chair that board, and the first woman to run a national Chicano/Latino organization, the Mexican American Legal Defense and Educational Fund.

There are other women like these. For example, in 1994 Remedios Diaz Oliver was a director of U.S. West and Avon Products (Roiz, 1994). Norma Cantu was the U.S. Department of Education's assistant secretary for civil rights. She emphasized early goal setting. Educator Juliet Villarreal Garcia was the president of the University of Texas at Brownsville. She believed college debating helped her most in her advancement. Perhaps she acquired critical thinking skills as she learned to debate.

In the late 1980s and early 1990s there was much feminist attention given to the "glass ceiling." The glass ceiling referred to the appearance that there was upward mobility for women. The emphasis was upon appearance. In fact, there was a clear barrier, a ceiling, that prevented women from climbing on the ladder of upward mobility. It should be noted that this invisible barrier to female upward mobility has color to it. One woman who has broken through the glass ceiling is Carolina Calderin, a Cuban, who is chief executive officer of Miami's Pan American Hospital. Latinas are working to break the glass ceiling for Chicanas. Teresa McBride is the chief executive officer of McBride and Associates, a computer service in Albuquerque, New Mexico, with over 100 employees and more than $20 million in sales. McBride stresses that Latinas own their own dreams and goals. It is the woman's vision and her own dream that must be the focus (*Vista*, 1994). Ann Casillas Chalker, owner of LFC Insurance Brokers & Agents in Los Angeles has made millions of dollars in insurance and real estate. Lordes G. Baird, who was born in Ecuador but raised in Los Angeles, has been a judge in the U.S. District Court for the Central District of California since 1992. Irma E. Gonzalez is a district court judge for the Southern District of California in San Diego. She and all the above women stress hard work.

Unique among leading Hispanic women in business are two sisters who followed different paths. Rosemary Barkett is the chief justice of the Florida Supreme Court in Tallahassee and was nominated by President Clinton to the U.S. Court of Appeals for the 11th Circuit. Her sister, Irma B. Elder, is the owner of a trio of car dealerships in Michigan. They consider it an advantage to have grown up in a multicultural and multilingual environment. Congresswoman Ileana Ros-Lehtinen represents Florida's 18th Congressional District. This Cubana worked as teacher and businesswoman. Nydia Velasquez represents the 12th District of New York. She grew up in the sugar cane fields of Puerto Rico, where her father was a cane cutter.

At the top of the legislative branch, three Latinas now serve in the U.S. Congress (Quiroz, 1994). One is Lucille Roybal-Allard who represents the 33rd District of California and is the first Mexican American woman elected to the House of Representatives. She is the oldest daughter of retired Congressman Edward R. Roybal, but is a leader in her own right. She advises young Latinas that staying in school is critical to upward mobility. Women should know they are not alone, and they need to build and manipulate their network.

There are also Latinas in the arts, like singer Gloria Estefan (Vista, 1994), who was selected Woman of the Year by the B'nai B'rith in 1992. Lisa Lisa is a top rock singer with her band called Cult Jam. Latina figures in sports are rising, and Mary Jo Fernandez and Nancy Lopez no longer stand alone at the top of women's tennis and golf. There are more actresses like Carmen Zapata; artists like California muralist Judy Baca; combined studio artists and muralists like Colorado's Carlota Espinoza, New Mexico's Delilah Montoya, and California's Yrina Cervantes; and independent movie and video producers like Solome Frances Espana. There are many writers, like Cherrie Moraga (Massachusetts), Sandra Cisneros and Gloria Anzaldua (Texas), Ana Castillo (Illinois); and rising poets like Gloria Alvarez (California).

CHICANAS HELPING TO HEAL THE NATION

Riots in large cities like Denver, Dallas, and Los Angeles scare some sexists and racists into behaving appropriately, but an underlying hostility can still be felt. Chicanas are sensitive to this and are available to give lectures and workshops to corporations, city governing bodies, classrooms, and community gatherings on how they see the world and what needs to be done to make it a better place. The few who profit from controlling and fragmenting social forces are being severely threatened with the "new world order," which includes sharing space with people of color, women, and the rest of the world. But the raza need educating also. Like racism, sexism has become institutionalized, a part of the socialization process of individuals. It has become internalized to the point where many feel a division of the genders is good and natural. This false sense of consciousness is referred to as the "colonized mind." Individuals are unable to see how their oppression functions and often blame themselves for their own misfortune.

Although Chicana feminists acknowledge free will and individual decision making, institutionalized discrimination is very real. Those with resources and privileges take advantage and abuse those without. The civil right movements, labor unions, and poor people's campaigns have been very effective at changing conditions in the United States; but even when Chicanas appear accepted by Anglos, they are accepted only as long as they are few in number, they do not act Chicano, or they act Chicano within settings that are prescribed as "acceptable." Outside of this setting, Anglos (even feminist Anglos) sometimes do not see la Chicana. As testimony is offered the many times Anglo men and women in academia have courted Chicana "input," obtained that input, but outside of the academic setting (in the mall or at a restaurant), they do not see or do not speak to the same Chicana. To be accepted, a Chicana must deny her own identity and take up the identity of the situation-prescribed norm. When a Chicana accepts the minority female norm, she accepts a gender role consisting of behaviors, rights, and responsibilities assigned to her by the dominant culture. When a Chicana accepts her cultural norm, she accepts that norm defined by both her own culture and that of the dominant culture, because the dominant culture influences her own culture. Herein lie the contradictions, those things frequently inconsistent with one another. A Chicana feminist defines her own role and struggles against accepting norms outlined or prescribed by others. She emerges with her own version of her own reality. Some Chicanas adhere to the dominant American Dream version of the norm. Others have a Chicano version of what that dream should be. Some are confused by the contradictions, but the feminist Chicana academic is very clear about her commitment to scholarship, its link to the community, and how this can contribute to healing the nation of the social ills of discrimination.

REFERENCES

Baca-Zinn, Maxine. 1975a. "Political Familialism: Toward Sex Role Equality in Chicano Families." *Aztlan: Chicano Journal of the Social Sciences and the Arts*, vol. 6 (Spring): 13–26.

———. 1975b. "Chicanas: Power and Control in the Domestic Sphere." *De colores*, vol. 1, no. 3, pp. 19–31.

Baca-Zinn, Maxine, et al. 1986. "The Costs of Exclusionary Practices in Women's Studies." *Signs: Journal of Women in Culture and Society*, vol. 2, no. 21: 290–303.

Blea, Irene I. 1981. "An Analysis of Mexican American Homemaking." Unpublished paper presented at 1977 National Association of Chicano Studies Conference, Claremont, California.

———. 1988. *Toward a Chicano Social Science*. New York: Praeger.

———. 1992. *La Chicana and the Intersection of Race, Class and Gender*. Westport, Conn.: Praeger.

Cotera, Martha. 1976. *Diosa Y Hembra*. Austin: Information Systems Development, pp. 24–29, 46, 49, 56–57.

Enriquez, Evangelina, and Alfredo Mirande. 1979. *La Chicana: The Mexican American Woman*. Chicago: University of Chicago Press, p. 17.

Figueroa Torres, J. Jesus. 1975. *Dona Marina: Una India Ejemplar*. Mexico, D.F.: B. Costa-Amic Editor.

Gomez Tagle, Silvia, Adrian Garcia Valdes, and Lourdes Grobet. 1985. *National Museum of Anthropology: Mexico*, translated by Joan Ingram-Eiser, pp. 27–30. Mexico, D.F.: Distribucion Cultural Especializada.

Harrington, Michael. 1963. *The Other American: Poverty in the United States*. Baltimore: Penguin.

Julip, Kay. 1994. *Vista*, vol. 9, no. 6. (February 9): 3.

Melville, Margarita B. 1980. *Twice A Minority: Mexican American Women*. St. Louis: C. V. Mosby.

Mora, Magdelina, and Adelaida Del Castillo. 1980. *Mexican Women in the United States: Struggles Past and Present*.

Orozco, Cynthia. 1986. *Chicana Voices: Intersections of Class, Race, and Gender*. Austin: CMAS Publications, pp. 11–18.

Quiroz, Joaquin. 1994. *Vista*, vol. 9, no. 6. (February 9): 8, 12.

Roiz, Carmen Teresa. 1994. *Vista*, vol. 9, no. 6 (February 9): 8–10, 12.

Trujillo, Marcella. 1975. "The Road to Canon: The Road to La Pinta." In *An Anthology of Chicano Literature*. Austin: Chicano Studies Center, March 12–16, p. 83.

Vista. 1995. Vol. 9, no. 6 (February 9): 18.

Latina merging her culture and spiritual beliefs in a more meaningful way on her wedding day.

7   Liberation of the Chicano Community

This chapter more clearly defines culture and further explores the cry for liberation and the process of social change in the Chicano community as the process of broadening the social space Chicanos can occupy. Social change is placed in the context of liberation from the oppression of domination by Eurocentric culture. It is assumed in this chapter that Chicanos and Chicanas have been conquered in war and restrained or otherwise limited in their ability to occupy space that is, at best, controlled by them and, at least, represented by them. The Chicano redefinition of social roles and relations applies to residential patterns, the kinds of jobs people can have, where they live, where they feel comfortable, and what kind of religion they can practice. This chapter reminds the student that indigenous culture is inherent in Chicano culture and that spirituality is one of its major contributions. Indigenous elements assist in defining a self-concept, a social character for Chicanos, just as racism and sexism are social characteristics of the dominant culture. The chapter outlines evidence of this double standard, change in the Chicano community, and how Chicano studies introduces Chicano concepts into the social sciences.

SOCIAL SPACE AS A CONCEPT

The general idea of social space has to do with allowing a population to exist physically, spiritually, and emotionally. Any community needs self-determination and the right to be its cultural "self." This right to social space has been denied Chicanos and other Latinos. In the United States social space is linked to dominant cultural characteristics, such as testing and/or competition. The prevailing assumption is that space is severely limited. There are only so many jobs, resources, classrooms, courses, and parking spaces to go around. In order to be fair, criteria have to be established so that only those who qualify can have access. This is most evident in higher education. Social space is hierarchical; those who rank highest, according to the criteria, are placed at the top and receive the most benefits because they are the best, the most qualified, the most worthy. To those socialized in this way of thinking, this behavior appears logical. Those at the bottom should be at the bottom because they do not meet the criteria as well as those at the top. Few question who developed the criteria in the first place, and why. Also in the structure are those who cannot compete because they have been preselected out of the process via tests that took place prior to the final selection. These people never get to take the final tests that ultimately lead to better jobs, better housing, the ability to take more courses at better institutions.

Chicanos and other minorities do not have the same cultural background as those who design the tests, and so they do not do well. It is the objective of some Chicanos to help define and design the tests, the test-taking process, and the rewards. Some Chicanos are not so accommodating, however. They want to be free from the system to create their own system, their own social space, and their own evaluations with their own questions. Those in control do not want to give up their positions. This places Chicanos at odds with Anglo-dominated society.

As outlined, in the 1960s Chicanos began to question the vehicles for getting to the top, and they began to talk publicly about the vehicles necessary to remain at the top. They did this in order to create more space, better space, and more freedom for their people. Those who stayed with an active program of resistance are generally studied as "the left." Others resisted the verbal arguments that were given to justify keeping Chicanos in their place but did very little to change the situation outside of giving voice to the conditions. Some dropped out. Others conformed to what the system demanded because the consequences of poverty were too overwhelming, while others chose to infiltrate the system to change it. In the 1990s, we can see the results of the different courses of action; and we can also see the inability of those at the top to share the space or conceive a society that is not constructed the way dominant U.S. culture now exists.

SOCIAL CHANGE

Especially for Chicanos, change and creating a new social space does not come without a high cost. Most violence and property crimes are a reaction to cultural control of the subordinate culture by the dominant culture, or are at least linked to it as a form of self-destruction or resistance. A frustrated population can easily be spurred to anger, suicide, self-hate, and open acts of aggression against the oppressor and themselves. This is especially true when the promise of the society is so drastically different from the reality confronting so many of its citizens. When equality, freedom, and justice are the major promises and those guarantees are not delivered upon, people seek change. Social change is especially demanded when members observe that there are patterns distinguishing those who have a better quality of life, better life chances than others. In short, from oppression and frustration comes resistance, from resistance comes violence. Where and how a society interrupts this process is up to those in power. Generally, the powerful resist the early warnings and prepare themselves for a very long battle.

Basically, there are two kinds of change: revolt, or revolution, and reform. Revolution is quicker. Reform takes a long time. The general consensus is that Chicanos and other minorities have tried to reform the society, and they have failed. The symptoms of those fed up with the system, those who have lost their patience, are that some have taken to acting out the rage in the form of gang violence, dropping out of school, of nonparticipation in elector politics. In imposed ignorance, in resistance, or because of simple inability and fear, they have failed to identify with the dominant social system, with the real culprit of their discontent. Some of those who are not afraid to continue the Chicano movement have gotten out on the streets to educate. They lend the Chicano Studies perspective to the social war in a desperate attempt to save Latino culture, Latino cultural productions and the Latino people.

Strengthening society means preserving Latino culture. Cultural productions manifest in the spiritual, social, psychological, and physical environment of the Chicano community as art, poetry, music, religion, and social institutions such as education and the family. Resistance is frequently a subject in Chicano culture because cultural productions do not exist without being affected by the dominant society's cultural values. They are reflections of forces that demean and degrade the community. Frequently, what is rendered is how the Chicano community deals with hopes, fears, and the objectives of life and death. In Chicano culture these productions appear as family structure and family relationships that place a high value on music, dance, cleanliness, marriage, children, education, the elderly, fiestas, and other days of significance. While waiting for change, most members of the Chicano community have remained spiritual, kind, loving, and artistic. However, the national media does not cover this side of Chicano life. I would contend that these positive coping mechanisms are what has kept the population from taking up arms. Nonviolence is the preferred form of struggle. These coping mechanisms appear in art, theater, poetry, music, and religious practices that are not widely supported by the dominant culture because they question, attack, and expose the underside of the dominant culture's ways of keeping themselves comfortable.

If the student of Chicano culture does not understand and is not tolerant of this critical aspect of the community, then that person should find more palatable things to study. Many areas of Chicano society need research and forms of resistance is just one aspect. Another is how so many Chicanos have managed to live very productive lives. I believe that some of the answers can be found in Chicano spirituality and the ability of the people to persevere, persist. This model is best understood in the analysis of their indigenous cultures and how they have survived cultural rapes.

INDIGENOUS CONTRIBUTIONS TO CULTURE SURVIVAL

Indigenous contributions are evident today in Chicano and other Latino cultures. For example, Chicanos tend to be Catholic, but they may not practice their religion by going to church every Sunday or on holy days of obligation, saying daily prayers, receiving holy communion, or otherwise behaving as Catholics. Most Chicanos baptize their children, get married, and get buried in the church. What else they do to preserve spirituality is interesting. Some people have home altars and images of the saints inside and outside their homes. They use Catholic religion at the same time that they use Indian herbs. They pray with the same rhythm indigenous people chant. Those who attend church and live Catholic lives also seek to make their spirituality more relevant to themselves by burning incense and serving special foods. Chicano culture has many indigenous foods, like the avocado. It has incorporated them into diets of corn, beans, dried meats, vegetables, and fruits. Traditionally, food preparation and spirituality have been in the women's domain, an essential domain. Its production and preservation are of the utmost necessity. Heriberto Garcia Rivas, author of *Cocina PreHispanica Mexicana* (1988), maintains that the interchange of food between Indians and Spanish Europeans created a *cocina mestiza*. This cocina, a blended cuisine, is a combination of indigenous food prepared in a Spanish style and European ingredients prepared in an indigenous style. The same can be said for spirituality.

Cross-cultural productions include cooking utensils, such as grinding and mixing instruments like the *metate, molcajete,* and *comal*. Certain flavors, vanilla and chocolate, and condiments, such as pepper and salt, are indigenous. Culinary contributions include the preparation of green and red chiles, salsa, squash, avocados, beans, potatoes, and spinach. Corn was first used in Indian kitchens. Certain meats, venison, fish, and beverages also first appeared there. Cacao, a variety of fruit drinks and juices, liquors (*pulque*), fruits such as papaya, pineapple, and bananas, herbs, mushrooms, cactus, seeds, and nuts were first prepared by women on Indian hearths. When combined these ingredients produce tamales, salsa, tostadas, enchiladas, burritos, tacos, and shrimp cocktails. They appear in corn tortillas, stews, soups, salads, and roasts in a festival of color that bursts into celebrations at fiestas and dinner tables across the nation. The conquistadors and the women and men who came with them, and after them, brought goats, wheat, fruits and fruit trees such peaches, pears, cherries, and apples. To add to the diet and to facilitate labor and travel, they also brought the horse, oxen, cows, pigs, and chickens. In the traditional indigenous culture of the area, some New Mexicans point with their lips, in the Navajo tradition. Many church and holiday festivals include a variety of Indian symbols, like the god's eye; but parishioners note that Catholic doctrine excludes indigenous religion and sometimes even interprets it as savage and unsophisticated.

Even though the general society has little knowledge of this, Southwest Chicanos are very able to discuss their Indian and Spanish traditions of child rearing, the blending that produced la Virgin de Guadalupe, *brujeria* (what we recognize as witchcraft), the healing art of curanderismo, baptism, confirmation, and beliefs in *la llorona* (the crying woman), ghosts, and spirits. Many Latinos know the complex system of health and healing, the supernatural, and good and evil as elements of religion that constitute a worldview somewhat consistent with, yet very different from, that of the Anglo Americans. All this must be considered by those wishing to produce a theory that explains the Chicano way of life. For those not familiar with these assumptions, there is Chicano Studies.

Increasingly this knowledge has been violated, bastardized, discredited, challenged, diluted, and separated, and it has been channeled into institutions rooted in the dominant society that exploit it for profit. This experience must also be taken into consideration when constructing a social change theory. Quite simply, Chicanos are, at worst, a conquered population; at best, they are an oppressed group of people, and they are resistant. Any social change theory must include a recipe for the direction and quality of change, or it will be but an empty mental exercise producing nothing of value for the social world.

Throughout the United States, there is an increasing involvement of professional Mexican Americans in the church, in education, and in the streets. Street theater, mariachi masses, television and radio programs are common. Everywhere there are prayers and calls for assistance in promoting good health, good jobs, racial justice, and peace in the world. Religion and spirituality allow individuals the ability to make sense of their world. They guide them in times of crisis. In the Chicano community spirituality is an intimate element of daily life. It does not end when individuals go home from church or go to work. This spirituality is both very indigenous and very Spanish. Spirituality also provides a vehicle for socialization by bringing family and friends together. It plays its first role in the Chicano experience when the individual is born, is still a baby and is baptized.

A major element of the baptism ritual is the very personal parental selection of compadres and comadres, male and female godparents, or sponsors. Participation in the ritual establishes a relationship between the child and the sponsors. The sponsors and the resulting relationship is referred to by the child as *padrinos*. The female sponsor or godparent is called *madrina*. Equally important is the relationship between the parents and the padrinos. To non-Spanish speakers the terms become confusing when compadres and comadres also play a role in marriage and the extended family structure. It does not make sense to them that so many people are involved. During illness, hospitalization, and personal crisis the large number of people involved is cumbersome and disturbing to hospital personnel. Usually, these people and their presence can be a factor in the healing process. Part of healing demands the right to practice culture. In the not-too-distant past indigenous medicine, which includes religion, was considered the work of the uncivilized and the work of the devil, especially on el Dia de los Muertos, when Indian food and altars were erected in honor of the dead. Today Chicanos observe el Dia de Los Muertos in gatherings that attract thousands of people. Religious reform in the Catholic church has been the form of social change most frequently chosen by Chicanos but there has also been a cultural revolution in other aspects of their life.

LIBERATION THEOLOGY

Attempts at reform have taken place in several social institutions. As has been mentioned, the Catholic church is one structure in which this has taken place. While many have left the church because the process is too slow, only a few Chicanos have openly called for an entirely different religious structure. Most have chosen to work within the Catholic church and have focused upon liberation theology as an ideological framework for simultaneous social and religious change. Social change via liberation theology is growing in popularity. Debates in Latin America have highlighted its introduction for years. Priests and church members have striven to make real the theories of governing Christianity there. Liberation theology is a form of nonelectoral politics that seeks to get the power of the Catholic church involved in lifting political and social oppression around the world.

Discussions with adherents of liberation theology note that the United States is a Christian country and that there is a clear connection between the empowerment of communities and Christianity. The definition of Christianity, then, becomes an issue. Chicanos have voiced discontent with the church; feminist nuns have charged that Christianity is male dominated and that only males can hold the highest offices. They cite as examples that only men can be priests and only a male can become pope. Many truly do not believe that God meant to differentiate according to gender. In addition, Christian behavior has had it own contradictions that have been founded in the politics of men. Male advocates of liberation theology note that there is room for Chicana liberation within the context of liberation theology. Yet, women becoming priests does not appear to be an important issue for them or for Chicana feminists. Mostly, Chicano women and men have struggled within the church to make it more responsive to Chicano concerns, arguing on the need for viable participation in ongoing religious rites, direct social services for Chicano poor, and more Spanish-speaking priests. Only a few have voiced a need for women to become priests, and only a few have questioned and confronted the power of the pope; and only a few note that Chicana nuns tend to do domestic chores and work with the poor, unlike Anglo nuns who teach school and have more influence over policy.

In protest many Chicanas and Chicanos have converted to other religions. Some of these are very fundamental ones. Those who have converted cite contradictions in the Catholic church and faith as major reasons. They put forth other reasons too, including that there is too much ceremony and ritual in the church. The priest plays too heavy a role, thereby keeping the people from forming and maintaining a direct relationship with God. The priests and the church structure interfere too much with what the people want to do. In contrast, the fundamentalist religions hold entire services in Spanish. They have

Spanish prayers, teachings, and songs. People are an integral part of the services, not just an adornment or audience. The new religions are also more expressive. People can testify before the group. They can ask questions, clap hands to music, cry, and pray out loud. They exhibit much dancing and joy in knowing that the Lord exists. People offer to pray for one another. They ask for prayer, and they touch and visit one another. In alternative churches, women have found new roles and new power. They are called sisters, and the men are their brothers. There is little or no hierarchy. Women testify at microphones, stand before an audience, lead prayers, preach, cite passages from the Bible, sing, and generally feel more fully a part of the services. In the non-Catholic churches sociopolitical awareness is manifested in the testimonies. Some Chicano activists feel there is potential for political activity here. Others feel there is not. The emphasis is on the Lord, not on this world. This is very much different from the Catholic church practices.

A sociological definition of religion extends that religion is a social institution structured to support accepted beliefs, procedures, norms, and values. These institutions are slow to change and are frequently linked to other institutions that support them, assist them, in guiding human behavior. For example, religion is linked to the family, economics, politics, and health. Émile Durkheim (1915) wrote that religion is necessary for a society, not only because it integrates values but because it is a crucial factor in sustaining social cohesion. This cohesion was disrupted in a most dramatic way when Chicanos and other church members charged the church with sexually molesting their children. The archbishop of Santa Fe, New Mexico, was charged with several counts of child molestation by three women. He resigned his post. Tom Perez got national T.V. coverage in early September 1993, when the gay activist from Boulder and Denver accused an Anglo priest of sexually molesting him for years. Yet, despite Chicana feminist criticism of the church's stand on birth control and abortion, many Chicanas continue to tolerate the Vatican dictates on their lives. These dictates maintain the status quo and support male-dominant norms.

A person continues being socialized, learning social roles, norms, and behaviors, throughout her/his life. Dominant Christianity and its ideology tell social participants that social arrangements are adequate, that they are how they should be, that they are natural. Chicanas do not agree with this. For the most part ideologies become cemented during the early socialization process. Some cultures separate spirituality from everyday life and the values of the people. Chicana feminists do not. Chicanas and Chicanos sometimes opine that U.S. Anglos have become spiritually void. Chicana feminists note that by internalizing patriarchal dominance, some Chicanos have lost their spirituality and respect for the natural and spiritual power of women. Ideologies can change, but unless a person has an intense desire or a significant event occurs, most people never think about what they have learned by being social participants. They take their knowledge for granted, as truth. If they are relatively comfortable, as Latino men are when compared to Latinas, they have little motivation to change, and they continue to live under a false assumption, a false consciousness, thinking that what they believe is fine.

Like other people, Chicanos do not think much about their own church history and the nature of the historical roots of their faith. Many are even unaware of their indigenous spiritual ancestors because they have come to feel ashamed of being Indian and because they know identifying with other oppressed people brings additional discrimination. Thus, they turn against their own indigenous history and may even discriminate against Indians, who may have Spanish surnames. Once, the ideological relationship between Chicanos and Indians is recognized, however, this distance shortens considerably, and the two entities embrace because, finally, the world makes sense.

Chicano activists who called for the implementation of liberation theology contrasted the wealth of the church with the poverty of the Chicanos who helped build that wealth. Church activists insist that the church should go beyond providing pastoral care. For example, Sister Rosa Martha, a U.S. Catholic nun born in Mexico, began to train and certify church members in San Bernadino, California, in techniques of community empowerment. Her life in the church became so unbearable that she sued the archdiocese and separated herself from the Eurocentric, male-dominated institution. In addition to the church's non-controversial activities in adoption, family counseling, providing food and lodging for the poor, Chicanos call for lifting racial oppression from the church's own structure. They want to move forward the cause of liberating Chicanos from the social clutches of a dominant white society. Relief from oppression is the focus of two important days in Chicano existence, Cinco de Mayo (May fifth) and el Diez y seis de Septiembre (the sixteenth of September). These days commemorating Mexico's struggle for liberation are days of prayer and celebration in some churches. Ironically, they are also days when Chicanos are most likely to encounter spiritual and political conflict.

Chicano religion and spirituality, like that of other cultures, is a system of shared Christian and Indian beliefs and practices built around the idea of natural and supernatural forces. Supernatural forces are used to explain that which is known and that which is unknown. Characteristic of the manifestation of spirituality is the notion of god or gods, the nature of the spirit life on earth, the water, the sky, the trees, the animals, and the afterlife. For Chicanos this may involve sweats, prayers, and rituals of a physical, psychological, and spiritual nature. This is a population that recognizes that ghosts exist, that one can be hexed by witches, that individuals have power; but not all Chicanos believe this. Some people identify more with their Indian heritage, and others with their European heritage.

Other things that affect religion and spirituality have to do with the relationship of individuals to their god. Religion and spirituality assist in defining relationships to earth, heaven, hell, purgatory, supernatural beings like the saints (who were human beings but now symbolize spiritual power), and the spirits of the living and the dead. For religious and spiritual needs, the Chicanos' god manifests in every element of life. The spiritual relationship is exercised when students study and take tests in college. It manifests when women bathe their children, in everyday work. Other elements of life intervene when status, low power, and low prestige are artificially bestowed, for they are given in differential amounts as social rewards to individuals. Religion and spirituality have helped Chicanos understand their place in the universe. All too frequently the intervening, man-made, variables have placed Chicanos in an adverse or secondary relationship to god and to other groups of people. This social space has affirmed the need for competition, has assisted in making Chicanos accept being poorer, having lower status, and lower power and prestige than members of the dominant society.

Chicana feminists are aware of this. Few have chosen to publicly struggle against it, as did Sor Juana Ines de la Cruz during the colonial period in Mexico. Most Chicanas are born into Catholicism and are aware of its highly bureaucratic nature, but they have not investigated their own Indian tradition or noticed that they more frequently identify with values that are consistent with male norms and values. Even when women dominate an area, such as the recruitment, training, and mentoring of nuns, the fundamental theology is dictated by men.

SOME EVIDENCE OF CHANGE

Both Chicano academics and nonacademics have placed priority on the need for social change in all institutions. Perhaps the biggest Chicano fear in seeking that change is that children will be absorbed by dominant U. S. values, that talented Chicanos with Chicano consciousness, and material resources will be lost to the community, and that the community will not be empowered. Their biggest hopes, perhaps, are that the community will become economically stable, that racism will end, and that Chicano people will be allowed to fully participate in the ongoing society without having to give up their culture or be on constant alert for racism, sexism, and class discrimination. It is difficult to envision what direction this culture will take, given the fact that for 150 years it has had to live with discrimination.

The study of Chicano traditional and popular culture is important because culture sustains people. It gives them shared knowledge and direction for meeting their objectives. Without culture people are empty, lost, and can become confused. Without cultural references, individuals become disoriented and depressed, even suicidal. The person without culture is not rooted, is alienated or disenfranchised, and has a difficult time relating beyond superficial platitudes. Populations in secondary social positions, especially, need culture for insulation against oppressive forces. For Chicanos culture is also extraordinarily important because it includes rites of passage from one phase of life to another. Those times in a person's life that symbolize passage from one status to another must be recognized because they inform people how to act. In Chicano society these include the birth ritual, baptism, beginning school, the first holy communion, confirmation, *quinceaneras*, graduation, and marriage and death rituals. All of these phases are marked by ritual, and in between them a lot can happen. The student of Chicano culture needs to keep in mind that Chicano culture is constantly changing from within, but it is heavily influenced by the dominant culture, its laws, it expectations, it rewards, and its punishment. Both Chicanas and Chicanos have contributed much to the study of culture. They have forced social scientists as well as everyday citizens to consider that racism, sexism, and class discrimination can all impact a group of people at the same time.

This is social reality, especially for Chicanas who need upward mobility, yet want to hold onto their culture. If a woman is not Christian and heterosexual, her reality can, indeed probably will, become complex, even more complex than for women who seek the American Dream of upward mobility. Women's quest is different from that of men. Society socializes its females to grow up and marry and live happily ever after on the salary the males will earn. It also socializes them to make men a social priority and economic asset. Women are not meant to directly enter the labor market, support themselves, and make other social contributions in the arts, politics, and science. They are, instead, meant to stimulate the labor market, indirectly, as consumers and producers of babies, future workers (Benson, 1969). This is changing and now even the U.S. automobile industry is making cars with women in mind (Julip, 1994).

The last chapter outlined Latinas, like Linda Alvarado, who had entered into business. Alvarado is Chicana, the director of two major corporations, and president of Alvarado Construction in Denver, Colorado. She is part-owner of the National League baseball franchise known as the Colorado Rockies. Patricia Salas Pineda is also Mexican American, director of Levi Strauss Associates, Inc., and general counsel for New United Motor Manufacturing in Oakland, California. Hers is a joint venture of General Motors and Toyota. Both she and Alvarado value cultural diversity.

The best industries for Chicanas/Latinas to work in are telephone companies. The company with the most female Hispanic corporate officers is Chicago-based American Information Technologies Corporation, Ameritec, the "Baby Bell that serves telephone customers throughout the Midwest." Ameritech employees Mary E. Aguina and Belen Acosta-Bradley, both Puerto Rican, rank among its vice-presidents. Nynex, US West, Pacific Bell, and the source of them all, AT&T, hire a high number of Latina employees. Latinas are well represented in banks and insurance groups. Sandra Cid, a Puerto Rican, is vice-president of human resources at Prudential. Chase Manhattan employee Maria Elena Lagomasino is the Western Hemisphere area executive. She has many international obligations.

Socialization messages are given and received in a multidimensional manner. They control Latina dreams and actual behavior, like sex and sexual orientation. Evidence of change is noted when some Chicanas and Chicanos go public about their lesbianism and homosexuality. This perspective can be seen in Chicano Studies where Chicana lesbian feminists do not adhere to the lifestyle, sexual desires, and homophobia of the general society. Their own culture does not support these contentions. Gays and lesbians note their responsibility to filter through the messages and create lives for themselves. It is society's responsibility not to interfere.

How humans manipulate through the social fabric to become what they are is not totally known, and this is an area ripe for social research. Research in this area would add much to the understanding of social change and cultural specific variables. Feminist scholars have analyzed how society brainwashes women into thinking they are incomplete and can only obtain social worth if they exist as the dominant version of what is defined as female by males, that is being blond, light skinned, blue-eyed, tall, and with a lean body. The ideal is to become a middle-class married woman, and have 2.5 children, keep the husband happy, and die. For the most part, Chicana socialization sustains the artificial importance and dominance of men; but it also includes the ideal Anglo model of what is considered an attractive or beautiful woman. If a Chicana does not fit this pattern, the consequence is low self-esteem and self-image and the notion that she has to settle for something less than the ideal. This has important ramifications for the Chicano community because men have received their own set of, often-times contradictory, values. From Anglo males they receive messages that Mexican and/or Indian men are less than men. Women of color expect men of color to provide what they think Anglo males provide for Anglo females, and minority men are expected to prove their manhood in some convoluted ways.

The truth of the matter is that sometimes the messages get mixed up for males and females. They produce peculiar adaptation behaviors that need to analyzed as such. More research is needed in this area, but for now it is sufficient to note that adaptation is a creative process. When people find mixed messages, they create their own interpretations and their own coping devices. La Chicana has done this very well, and there exists a group of women in academia who have made a lifetime commitment to documenting this endeavor. They work in the area of Chicana/Latina Studies. They have not only concentrated on how female socialization produces a female norm, but note that at the same time, women are the producers of children and the producers and consumers of goods and services. Academic Chicana feminists produce knowledge. They have published, and they can be found on the university and college campuses of the United States. There are not very many of them, and this keeps them isolated. Their work focuses on how prescribed social roles rarely bring all the status, power, and prestige that women believe they will gain by being traditional women and how these elements are not ascribed if they deviate from traditional norms. The social costs are high. Fantasies and dreams, especially in marriage, typically remain unrealized, not only for women but also for men. Nevertheless, Chicano people, like most Americans, remain addicted to the American Dream, its teachings, its assumptions, and its promises of "the good life." Why this is true despite discrimination needs further research. It may have something to do with the "colonized mind," spirituality, or the human temperament. Other funda-

mental questions include why Chicanas, who are not born into the Anglo physical norm, adhere to those social norms; or do they? How they conceive and
cope with discrimination has not been studied in any real depth; nor has why
more Chicanas do not marry out of the Chicano community as a form of upward
mobility. These questions have to do with social change and the fact that women
in Chicano culture have changed, thus changing culture.

CHANGING PARADIGMS

What, then, has been the impact of social change on the Chicano community,
and what has been the impact of the study of Latino culture, marriage patterns,
art, religion, and spirituality on the advancement of the Chicano community and
social sciences? How has Chicano Studies been able to make an impact? What
makes this study different from other social sciences? What is the academic Chi-
cana/Chicanos' connection to scholars in other fields. These are all questions
that Chicanas and Chicanos in the social sciences have not had time to investi-
gate because they have been too busy trying to stay alive in the academic arena,
an arena still characterized by negativism and conflict.

I contend that more often than not cultural realities (including male-female
differences) are rooted in perceptions and in degrees of social power, rather
than in natural ability and actual impact. There is a false reality that is not linked
to the natural order of things, and it can be changed. Thus, Marx's emphasis on
false consciousness and Durkheim's concentration on natural progression, noted
in earlier chapters of this text, are integrated to establish saliency in both perspectives and also to create a synthesis, a new thought, a new entity, a new paradigm. In adopting and adjusting these integrated perspectives, insisting on
another way of looking at reality, Chicano Studies has created new paradigms
over the course of the last 25 years. These multicultural paradigms are now
being adopted by universities across the nation. Those universities having to
adopt Chicano Studies models, however, have not given credit to the achieve-
ments of Chicano Studies and are excluding Chicanos from the leadership in
creating new programs, areas of study.

The Chicano activist should be interested in what the social sciences produce,
their cultural productions. The construction and analysis of a scientific study of
the nature of a group of people tell much about how the world is viewed, constructed, and sustained as the truth, or forced to change, in the eyes of those
who legitimize it. In short, social scientists assist in shaping and maintaining an
ideology, a belief system, the doctrines and convictions of the society, and they
frequently resist change because it is not in their interest.

Those who resist change will not acknowledge that women are strong in Chicano culture. They are strong as cultural and decision-making symbols, and
they are strong physically and spiritually. Even in folklore women are the leading cultural symbols: la virgin (virgin), la llorona (crying woman), la bruja
(witch), la curandera (healer). Chicano men are highly resilient. Cultural and

historical social conditions have demanded that both females and males develop strong characters and work hard. Both men and women value home life. My study of Bessemer and casual observances of women in many other Chicano neighborhoods reveal that heterosexual women are not hesitant to work alongside men in maintaining their home, creating a garden, raising children. After working long hours during the week (longer than most white men for the same pay), Chicano men do not hesitate to do physical work around their homes; and, increasingly, more and more men are becoming involved in child rearing. Chicanos are predominately members of the working class, but there is a sizable middle-income group. Although Chicano earnings are less than that of Anglos, they have an internalized work ethic somewhat stronger than the dominant work ethic. Chicano males have endured discrimination similar to that of African American men. Discrimination works to emasculate them, to make them feel inferior by denying them jobs, the symbol of U.S. masculinity. This tactic has worked to some degree, and Chicano males frequently abandon women and children in search of something else that will legitimize them. A new direction is called for by Chicanas, one that has different expectations from men, one that has female input.

Nevertheless, men have adopted and have sustained preferential positions and treatment in Chicano culture. This tendency did not begin with Anglo political imposition, but was one of the last straws in sustaining male identity. The more urbanized and the more assimilated Chicanos become, the more the power differential between Chicano women and men increases. For U.S. born Chicanos, the form that this has taken recently is more American than Mexican. Even at birth Chicano females and males do not start out the same. Boy babies are still preferred. After birth the genders experience different roles that manifest in different life chances.

The dominant society will have to adopt different expectations for Chicanos. Put simply, Chicanos and other racial and ethnic minorities are not all living down to a standard. Dominant Americans will have to accept that Chicanas are fluent in two cultures, two languages, and more than one class and that they very often outperform them. There are many Chicanos, unfortunately, who are afflicted by the ills of, the symptoms of, discrimination: poverty, drugs, gang warfare, teen pregnancy, crowded housing, bad health, uncleanliness, and all the other stereotypes. These, however, are not the majority. The Bessemer study revealed what other studies have also shown: that the majority of the population are gainfully employed, are raising healthy children, and are trying to gain upward mobility. A good many community members have excelled within the dominant system and have been rewarded for being gifted. They are rooted in their command of the Spanish language, in their Latino identity, and they are fluent in English and in the dominant culture. In short, they are culturally literate. The dominant and Chicano societies do not hear much about these members of the population because good news about Chicanos does not sell newspapers.

REFERENCES

Benson, Margaret. 1969. "The Political Economy of Women's Liberation." *Monthly Review*, vol. 21, no. 4 (September): 37.

Blea, Irene I. 1992. *La Chicana and the Intersection of Race, Class, and Gender*. Westport, Conn.: Praeger.

Durkheim, Émile. 1915. *The Elementary Forms of the Religious Life*. New York: Macmillan and Free Press. Originally published in 1897.

Garcia Rivas, Heriberto. 1988. *Cocina PreHispanica Mexicana*. Mexico, D.F.: Coleccion Panorama.

Julip, Kay. 1994. *Vista*, vol. 9, no. 6 (February 9).

8 Linking Theory to Practice

This chapter outlines how Chicanos understand themselves and notes that the term "struggle" is a constant in Chicano activism, in Chicano Studies, and Chicano literature. This is because there is, indeed, a power struggle going on between the disempowered Chicano and those in power. The chapter's focus is on that multidimensional struggle and challenges readers to expand upon the work of scholars. The chapter continues to concentrate upon the impact of challenging and changing assumptions within academia, the Latino community, and the general society. This chapter concentrates on how knowledge is disseminated to the student and to the community, through perspectives in the study of women, politics, and the criminal justice system. Applied research, putting knowledge to work to improve society, and the work of the social activist scholar is also emphasized.

CHALLENGING THE DISSEMINATION OF KNOWLEDGE

Chicanos have traditionally been analyzed via the institutional approach. It is suggested that another approach, that of the utilization of academic space, be applied. This, of course, includes concentration upon social-historical, physical, psychological, and spiritual space. The concept of space, here, has to do with taking up room in the world psyche while asserting a definition of the population's territory, reiterating the self-evident but often forgotten truth that the United States is only one of many Latino countries in the Americas and hence cannot refer to itself as America. In fact, the United States of America defines very little—there are united states throughout Latin America.

The distance between where Chicanos are in society and where they want to be (where they live, where and how they work, how society arranges places re-

Jose Angel Gutierrez speaks to students about linking theory and practice, community to course work, in the early 1970s.

served for them, how uncomfortable these arrangements are, the conflicts this order causes, and the need to be free of this) is great. Chicanos know that social space is much less fluid than most would like to believe. This is why some scholars of color have compared race relations in the United States to the rigid caste system of India (Cox, 1970; Barrera 1979). Unlike the caste system, however, democracy is hypothetically more willing to allow people to excel, achieve, increase in status. For people of color, excelling has its price, and not all can excel and be culturally salient. Caste is more like a rank-given, ascribed status with no hope of change. "Minority" status, despite the large number of people of color, is more like a station in life with a glimmer of hope for change, but it is still rigid. Some have placed hope for change in education; but this is inappropriate because discrimination exists in education as well as in politics, economics, the health system, the criminal justice system, the media, religion, and in families simultaneously. These all act as a united force to target the person of color.

Because of this displaced hope for social change, one of the first social spaces that was challenged by Chicanos was education. Going to school takes up a lot of a young person's time, space. Therefore, understanding the relationship of the educational system to the list of variables listed above is important. Generally, Chicano scholars, social activists, and politicians have criticized the educational system and have testified that schools were/are not educating Chicano children in a way that empowers both them and the community. The schools are charged with not teaching students skills by which to learn and retain culture, get jobs, develop individual talents, and change the social circumstances. This contention assumes that the schools should have the interests of students and the community at heart, and that schools should build skills that allow children to grow up to be healthy adults and generally participate in their communities, Chicano communities included.

Bessemer Chicanos realized the disparity between the ideal and the real objectives of education in 1978–1979. The objectives were to Americanize, to teach dominant American culture in order to empower dominant American society. Chicanos who had gone to school had not been taught to respect their community and culture, and sought to make sure the experience was not repeated in their children's lives and in the lives of Anglo children. Critics of the educational system claimed that discrimination based on race, segregation, and inferior quality of schools, texts, teachers, and teaching approaches had been the barriers. In the late 1970s and to a great extent today sexism was/is not an issue for Chicano educational activists.

Because of their experiences, Chicanos have no reason to trust the educational system and the people who work in it. Individual schools have recognized this, and they have tried to change; but, for the most part, Chicano scholars still have a difficult time obtaining good information about drop-out and graduation rates because these rates, when compared, mark the success or failure of the school. It is important for the researcher to note that a non-finding should be treated as a finding. It means something to find nothing. The task of the researcher is to discover what is missing and why it is not available. Perhaps it is symptomatic of a coverup.

When conducting a community study, it is important to place education, and all the social institutions, within a social-historical context relevant to Chicanos. Few educators understand Chicano resistance to engaging in a process that demeans, devalues, and denies their historical experience because they do not see the system as doing this. In Bessemer, information on the status of Chicanos in Pueblo District 60 was basically inconsistent, erratic, unreliable, and sometimes evasive (1990). Few residents and professionals knew of the historical role of the CF&I in providing education for the community. In the late 1970s the high school drop-out rate for Latinos was high. Even though some national progress has been made on the high school graduation rate, the drop-out rate for Chicanos is still too high.

In the 1970s only three of ten Hispanos/Chicanos aged 25 and older had completed at least four years of high school (U.S. Bureau of the Census, 1993). Less than one in 20 had completed four or more years of college. In 1980, about four in ten Hispano/Chicanos had completed four or more years of high school and one of every 13 had completed four or more years of college (see Table 8.1). In 1990, only half of the population had at least a high school diploma. One in 11 had earned a bachelor's degree. It should also be noted that the Mexican-origin population had a high school educational attainment level (44.2 percent) just below those of Dominican-Republic origin (42.6 percent). Hispanos and a college degree rate of 6.2 percent was also below that of Dominicans (7.8 percent). In 1990, nearly 10 percent of the Hispano population had received a bachelor's degree or higher. About 20 percent of Spaniards and South Americans had received a bachelor's degree or higher compared with only 6 percent of Mexicans. South Americans and Spaniards had high school graduation rates of 70.7 and 76.7 percent respectively.

The schools are not only designated to serve people in a certain physical space, they are designed to serve them in a specific social space. Problems with these boundaries have been outlined for well over 30 years and will not be discussed here in order to save space for other less discussed, but equally impor-

Table 8.1
Percentage of Hispano/Chicano High School and College Graduates, 1970–1990

	High School	College
1970	30	5
1980	40	7.7
1990	50	9

Source: U.S. Department of Commerce, Bureau of the Census. "We the American Hispanics," November, 1993, pp. 4–5.

tant, topics. One of those topics maintains that when the boundaries are not adhered to, those stepping outside of them will suffer negative consequences. Some of the consequences have been outlined in the discussion of Chicano Studies and the difficulties it has encounted on university campuses, but they are not limited to the discipline that tried to change university culture and curriculum. Bilingual education and other similarly progressive programs have endured the same negativity. This problem is generational. Many Chicano adults have gone to the schools their children now attend. Some desire to live in the same neighborhood and pass on its tradition to the next generation of children. Today, many schools are plagued with property crimes, violence on campus, handguns, and drugs. In 1994, for example, some Los Angeles area schools have taken away lockers in order to prevent the storage of drugs and handguns. Some schools have resorted to requiring school uniforms in order to promote higher educational achievement. In the 1970s, a few Bessemer residents recognized the dominant society's expectations of low educational achievement for their children, but parents still aspired for a high school degree for their children. In 1994, that aspiration was consistent with the national aspiration; it had now increased to a college degree.

THE BATTLE OF IDEAS

When scholars terminate their studies they present their findings through various mechanisms. This can be done in the form of a term paper, a master's thesis, a Ph.D. dissertation defense, a published article, a book, a video tape, or a movie. There are other ways that Chicano research is presented in art, music, and poetry. Scholars and students gather in class, in conferences, at meetings, and in consciousness-raising groups to share knowledge. Scholarship can manifest in laws and other policies. What is done with the findings, the information, the knowledge, dictates where and how the research is presented. If it is being presented in the classroom, the teacher or professor may require a written and/or an oral report. This process in the classroom is most powerful because it gets lots of information to the impressionable minds of the youth. Thus, there is a struggle over what is researched, what is taught, who teaches, and how it is taught.

Chicanos and Chicanas engage in this struggle at the lower levels of the public hierarchical educational structure, and they struggle in higher education, in undergraduate and graduate programs. I have discussed how la Chicana's major academic contribution has been a multifaceted theoretical perspective on the intersection of race, class, and gender, and how this contribution was made possible by Chicanas' struggle to integrate this perspective into Chicano Studies and Women's Studies. Through this effort, la Chicana has combined her experiences to emerge with a multifaceted analysis that goes further than separating the variables and analyzing where and when they manifest. Chicanas and other women of color have concentrated on how and why they interact, synthesize, or mix to formulate a reality.

Until the very late 1980s college and university campuses that studied issues of gender tended to focus on gender analysis as the experience of white women. This worked against the dissemination of what was/is known about la Chicana. Women's Studies not only placed a lot of attention on Anglo women, it studied male-dominated industrial societies and what they did to white women; but industrialization had a further negative impact on American Indian and Mexican American women in that it not only fragmented the family work unit, but also severely disrupted the culture, devaluing the language and knowledge base via its introduction of exchange capital. During industrialization, the average Anglo woman could not compare in standard of living, status, and authority with that of the average white man. For Chicanas there was no comparison with white women, and they protested vehemently to industrialization (Padilla, 1993). This lack of comparison to white women is also true of indigenous women (Green and Porter, 1992). Early industrialization and Americanization efforts destroyed a way of life and forced many Native Indians and Chicanos to move from their aboriginal lands to villages, reservations, small towns, and cities.

Anglo families were commonly torn apart by industrialization. Women left their homes to beg, to be exploited in factories, or to become prostitutes. Women and children were preferred workers because they were considered docile, easy to control, and less likely to strike over low wages and poor working conditions. When and if they were allowed to work, Chicanas and Chicanos entered the labor force with similar stereotypes, but with lower wages than whites. They encountered the terrors of hierarchical management and racism on the job and were considered even more stupid than white women and children.

More affluent Anglo and Hispano women did not have to work in factories, yet they shared forms of discrimination with impoverished and working-class women. They could not vote. Anglo women were seldom allowed careers; Chicanas did not dare think of careers. Anglo women had no control over family or personal property, and were less likely to be educated. Early Chicanas lost some of this control after the U.S. war with Mexico and the appropriation of what is now known as the Southwest into U.S. territory. This was so hateful that former Mexican women despised the Anglo who, in turn, hated them (Padilla, 1993). Indian women, for the most part, escaped some of this, but they were subjected to different forms of sexism and racism via the poverty of their imprisonment on reservations. As young children they were taken from their families for long periods of time and forced into American Indian schools. Indian women were once respected in their traditional cultures as providers of wisdom and guidance. Under American rule they found themselves held in disdain by those with European views. Native American women and Chicanas have relived this when white feminists write and talk as if womanhood was, or is, a universal experience.

Discrimination, for both Chicanos and Chicanas, is an ever-constant, ever-changing social control mechanism that keeps people in their place by changing as the society changes. It exists because it functions to support the Anglo American values of competition, significant profit margins, and domination. In the study of Chicanas and Chicanos there has been a tendency to accept the view that race transcends class, that race matters more than class. Gender transcends both class and race. What is important in the discussion of woman of color is not which comes first or overrides the other, but that discrimination is experienced—sometimes based on race, sometimes based on gender, sometimes based on class, and most of the time based on all factors at the same time. This makes the analysis complex and sometimes confusing; but the confusion is not necessary if the process is understood as victimization via intersecting variables.

Victimization can be better understood if the dominant Western thought process is briefly reviewed as binary and hierarchical, consisting of stratified binary opposition ranging from low to high in value, somewhat like a ladder with a line painted down the center. For example, there is a tendency to think in categories exemplified by good-bad, in-out, black-white, up-down, male-female. If individuals are in categories that have less value or worth (less money, less education, less political power), then they get ascribed less. They are relegated to negative value. This negative space generates little money, little access to power, status, privilege, and prestige. Those in power do not want the masses to know this. In fact, those in power have accrued so much privilege over hundreds of years of discrimination that they might not even recognize it themselves. It is my contention that society's poor and disenfranchised have recognized the forces at work in our social system, and this is why there is conflict and violence in the United States.

POLITICAL CHALLENGES

In the past, non-Chicano social scientists consistently contended that Chicanos experienced lack of upward mobility because of failure to organize and work hard. But Chicanos have worked hard. They have organized and struggled as part of the U.S. labor movement for union jobs and better working conditions; but they want more than upward mobility. They want a fundamental change in the social structure. In the 1970s Chicano scholar Raymond A. Roco (1976) documented that Chicanos have had a long history of organization. In 1994, the list of organizations was so long that booklets and directories were published, and Chicano organizations and Chicano politics is an area of specialization within the Chicano Studies curriculumn. It has been revealed that non-Chicano social scientists have a too narrow conception of what constitutes organization. They do not recognize that, like African American organizations (Du Bois, 1967), many Mexican American organizations serve purposes other than that of political organization. They fulfill a multiplicity of social, religious, economic, and educational functions at the same time.

In the 1960s, Chicano emphasis was on both electoral and nonelectoral politics. In the 1970s, nationalism, centering on Chicano ethnicity, was the dominant thread in Chicano politics. During this time the Raza Unida party was perhaps the most nationalistic Chicano political organization. Its seeds were planted at the Cabinet Committee Hearings in October 1967 in El Paso, Texas. It sought to work within the dominant political structure by changing the color of its face, by involving more Chicanos at the organizing levels, and by supporting the election of Chicano candidates. The nationalistic movement heavily influenced Chicano politics throughout the United States in a way that can still be felt today. Although those adhering to a purely nationalistic ideology were few, it cannot be denied that most, if not all, Chicano political activity has taken this form of activity to some degree or another.

In the 1980s, Chicano political participation via the electoral process got more attention but the nonelectoral efforts continued. The decade was called the "Decade of the Hispanics," but very few experienced upward mobility and/or a decrease in discrimination. Nonelectoral political activists continued in organizing efforts at the grass-roots level around issues like empowering women, North American Free Trade Agreement (NAFTA), various health and criminal justice issues, mental services, education, reform within the Catholic church, and making public education relative to Chicanos.

In Bessemer, the Chicano Democratic Caucuses have existed since the 1970s. In Denver a similar organization, which began in the 1980s, is called Hispanics for Colorado. In New Mexico the Hispanic Roundtable sought to empower raza. Throughout the Southwest similar organizations are composed of registered Democrats who have become the most visible group in their communities. As in Bessemer, these organizations have had the objective of empowering the Chicano community by focusing upon political, educational, and employment issues. Many of these organizations have been active at the state, and even the federal, levels and have been heavily criticized by other Chicano organizations with similar views as being too conservative, Eurocentric, and nonrevolutionary.

The Republican party is popular among Chicanos as is the Democratic party, but it is less visible in Chicano communities. From time to time, it has featured Hispanics. The Republican party has had associations with Chicanos for some time. In Bessemer, the southern Colorado region, and in New Mexico, as examples, many Chicanos continue to vote Republican. In the 1970s, in Bessemer, the party's involvement had been very little and had met with limited success in obtaining the Chicano vote. But it can be said that the Raza Unida party was successful for it raised Chicano consciousness.

In the late 1970s, Bessemer informants felt that the Raza Unida party had lost credibility because it failed to win elections. But the party had a substantial impact in Texas, especially in Crystal City, where it had phenomenal success due to the grass-roots efforts of Jose Angel Gutierrez. Only a few Raza Unida members contended that winning elections was not the objective of the party. One objective was to inform the two-party system that it was not addressing Chicano issues and that a vote for a Raza Unida candidate was actually a protest vote. It should be mentioned that many members of organizations like the Chicano Democratic Caucus were once active in the Raza Unida party. They departed from the party because of a male, close-knit clique that would not share the leadership. Rivalry among the men broke out, and the party was disempowered. Of the many who dropped out, a sizable number did so because they wanted to be part of the decision-making process. In late 1978 and 1979, the Raza Unida activity was sometimes visible in the Pueblo, Colorado, barrio on the east side of town largely because of the efforts of Eddie Monture, but rarely in Bessemer. In the 1980s, it disappeared in most parts of the Southwest.

Most Chicanos in the 1990s see nationalism issues as limiting the role of raza, especially women, and not being broad enough to bring about significant social change outside of ethnic politics. Conformity is still an option in the 1990s, but discrimination is at a new height. Racial incidents increased, as did civil discontent. In the 1992 elections, 62 percent of Hispanic voters voted for Governor Bill Clinton of Arkansas as president of the United States. In 1994, about half of the population surveyed indicated that the president was doing a good or excellent job of governing the nation. According to *Vista* magazine (1994) there were signs that Chicanos were not impressed with Clinton, at best they rated him as fair. Fewer than 10 percent thought Clinton had done an excellent job but 12 percent believed he had done an excellent job of appointing Hispanics to high office. Clinton did appoint former mayor of San Antonio, Texas, Henry Cisneros, and Federico Pena, former mayor of Denver, Colorado, as secretary of housing and urban development and secretary of transportation respectively. Cubans, who favored George Bush in 1992, were the Hispano population least impressed by the Clinton administration. Only 5 percent gave the president a rating of excellent (*Vista*, 1994).

Chicano community political participation cannot be separated from academia and political participation at the local, regional, and international levels. It is interesting that a larger faction does not advocate the overthrow of the entire U.S. economic and political system. Instead, most organizations and individuals agree that the best political route to take in promoting change is that of reform, not revolution. Chicanos simply want to retain their culture, have an opportunity to compete fairly, be able to celebrate their community, and end discrimination. They want higher rates of political participation, more money for education, and a change in the curriculum. They want to be healthier, and they want a decrease the number of Chicano criminals.

CHALLENGING THE CRIMINAL JUSTICE SYSTEM

In the 1990s crime is a major issue. Being a person of color renders individuals a good chance of encountering the law, being sent to prison, and appearing on death row, especially if a white, Anglo male or female is killed by a person of color. This is one of the reasons the Rodney King, Damon Williams, and O. J. Simpson trials are so important. In the King trial white Los Angeles police officers were charged with beating an African American male. In the Williams trial an African American male was charged with beating an Anglo male during the Los Angeles riots that were sparked by the beating of Rodney King. Both incidents were recorded on video tape, and both trials were very public. For months the Chicano community of Los Angles, as well as those in other cities, debated, predicted, and awaited the results. In the end the verdicts were achieved and debated, but not without an extraordinary amount of tension and attention by the communities of color. In summary, the communities of color were watching, fearing a double standard of justice, making sure it was not being practiced. A stressful peace resided, especially in Los Angeles, until the O. J. Simpson case once again placed race as a leading issue in the national media.

In 1994, in Los Angeles the leading killer of young people was the handgun. As in other cities, gangs, guns, and drugs kill people of color at alarming rates. Most of the victims are young, generally male, under the age of 21, and killed by members of their own ethnicity and/or race. They all have mothers, sisters, grandmothers, aunts, madrinas and padrinos (godparents), other relatives, lovers, girlfriends, and boyfriends who care for them. When a young person is killed the entire network is victimized. Often this network strikes back. Funeral expenses, burial plots, headstones, flowers, clothing, and songs mean a minimal cost of $5,000 to $8,000 per funeral. Most of these service providers are white. Women and children are especially traumatized, left with emotional scars and messages that tell them that men are violent, they kill, and they leave women behind with bills to pay and messes to clean up. The cost to society has not been calculated, but it must include the loss of a worker's wages, the creativity of an artist, the community empowerment of a social worker, professor, doctor, scientist, or engineer. Yet, many still see the problem of gangs, guns, and drugs as a criminal issue, something that needs to be legislated, laws that need to be enforced, and persons who must be incarcerated. Some effort is being made to redefine the problems as health or social service issues, but few can surpass their colonial and colonized mentality to see another approach. By no longer assessing blame, guns can be characterized as dangerous products that kill, just like cigarettes and drugs. They are harmful, especially, to the health of women, children, and young adults. U.S. government officials note that every two hours a child dies as a result of a gun. The wounded are disfigured and traumatized for the rest of their lives. What is not revealed is that for those close to the victim the psychological violence is a constant reminder that few care enough to end the physical violence.

Once in a while protests against violence are seen. It may appear that most Chicano activism is in the form of protest, but it is not. Thirty years of protest, threats, and pressure have not cured society of a double standard of justice. In the African American cases involving the beating of Rodney King it took a riot, several court cases (including that of Damon Williams) with several attorneys and experts, community pressure, and an abundance of national media attention to highlight the double standard. A growing number of Chicanos and African Americans have permeated the criminal justice system and the media in an attempt to change the definition of some crimes. They seek change from within, working as criminal attorneys, judges, parole and probation officers, social workers, film producers, and news broadcasters. Some favor the legal route, like Mat Perez, who sued the FBI for practicing racial discrimination and won.

Interaction with the criminal justice system is differentiated along class lines, and it can be said that every Chicano who has an encounter with the law is an activist of some sort. Anglos, especially those with wealth, have fewer negative experiences with the criminal justice system. When they make contact with law officials the reason for contact and duration of the experience is shorter, different, and more positive. The poorer person or the person of color will, generally, more frequently have the experience of being a suspect or an offender than a person needing protection, information, or assistance. The National Association for the Advancement of Colored People (NAACP) and numerous other studies have documented that the poor and people of color receive more guilty verdicts, longer sentences, and higher fines in the criminal justice system. More people of color go to jail. These findings are directly dependent on at least three factors: 1) the money a person has to hire a competent attorney; 2) the network of influential persons who can assist the individual; and 3) what that person represents to the establishment—the social value and worth of the individual or the social group the individual represents.

This finding is tied into the concept of space. The dual standard of justice keeps people in their prescribed social space. Chicanos must work to make immediate corrections in the criminal justice system because of the severity of the punishments they receive. They have looked toward those that govern the United States to accomplish this and have found little assistance. Many people of color no long trust the governing agencies and note that it is asinine to ask the oppressor to address and remedy what keeps her/him in her/his position of power. Some do not view government officials as having final responsibility for these kind of social decisions. That responsibility belongs to the people who elect these officials. The belief that government is nonresponsive is based upon experience rooted in Chicano history: the violation of the international Treaty of Guadalupe Hidalgo; racist, sexist policies that negatively affect Chicanos; and international policies that affect Spanish-speaking, third world countries. Over the years those holding these opinions have increased in number. Yet, a few Chicanos, and many more Anglos, believe in the saliency of the current governing structure and that a policy to eradicate racism and sexism can be legislated and implemented. Yet, such a policy has been in place for over 30 years.

BATTLING THE STANDARD

It is not surprising that so many are so angry. Poverty, gang violence, drive by shootings, riots, property crimes, a Eurocentric curriculum, a hierarchical structure, double standards of justice, and the accompanying anger make sense to Chicano scholars. They are manifestations of oppression, of the conquered being controlled by the conqueror. It is of interest that when people are ultimately disempowered, they do not have to be actively oppressed by outsiders.

They oppress themselves. Some of this is done to numb the emotional pain caused by the situation, the pain created by the tightness of the social and physical space reserved for the conquered. The conquered recognize that the conditions of that space are forced upon them, members of their families, their neighbors, their people in this third world. They recognize they are entrapped in lifestyles, not defined by them. The legacy of being conquered breeds frustration, and continued frustration breeds violence.

To further understand this, look at the difficulties encountered in placing Chicano students and Chicano Studies on U.S. college and university campuses. The intense resistance to getting updated knowledge to interested students on campus has been phenomenal. Those who try to integrate to achieve a more representative student body and a more accurate curriculum immediately find two guidelines within hierarchical structures: one affecting "minorities" and one affecting others. The double standard includes different interpretation of rules, expectations, status, power, and prestige for Anglo men, Anglo women, the poor, men of color, and women of color. Specific jobs, social opportunities, and legal protection are available to each; but they are more available to those with the higher status, higher prestige, and higher value, or social worth. College and university campuses, elected offices, and the decision-making end of the criminal justice system are not considered places for Mexicans/Chicanos/Latinos to be. This not only includes their physical presence, but their individual and collective life views, morals, ethics, values, indigenous philosophy, art, music tradition, and spirituality. Further, those seeking to keep Chicanos out adhere to the fact that Chicanos are not the elite of American society. In fact, they are cited as the most deficient. Those seeking to keep Chicanos in their place have evidence to prove Chicano populations deviate from normative American reality. Sometimes they define the reality through their silence. The more verbal cite low educational attainment rates, low political participation, low incomes, low levels of health, and high criminal justice rates. To make the Chicano struggle for liberation from a double standard even more difficult, those in control dictate the arenas in which these type of discussions take place: in the board rooms where they are the majority, on the jobs where they supervise, in the classrooms where they teach, in the courts where they judge.

Often people of color turn against one another. In my late 1970s Bessemer study, various sources documented that the Colorado Fuel and Iron Company, the dominant employer in the region, had historically used racial and ethnic minorities against one another as strike breakers. Antagonisms out of work situations grew because institutionalized hiring practices undercut one ethnic group's wages by creating a substitute pool of cheap labor in another ethnic group. White ethnic workers resisted and protested because they saw a second group of immigrant European workers as unfair competition. Rather than express hostilities toward the controlling employer, the employed white ethnic group acted out against the more vulnerable and visible immigrant group. Both populations harbored hostilities and transferred them onto one another, and finally onto the

Mexican. A historical cycle of distrust, dislike, and misdirected hostile transference was set into motion between, and among, populations. Job manipulation and competition entrap people in multifaceted cycles of discrimination that manifested in some negative qualities of life in the community (Blea, 1988).

The student of Chicano communities needs to research the patterns described above in her/his own community. Students need to be careful when using the immigrant model to analyze Chicano issues. Chicanos were not immigrants. Their population has been added to by immigration. Students need to know that occasionally Chicanos are allowed to administer Chicanos, but these administrators are usually kept in subordinate positions and/or are accepted as nonthreatening to the Anglo elite. The Bessemer study demonstrated that Pueblo city councilman and mayor, Ben Marquez, was seen by Chicanos as filling this position. Chicano activists and a group of Bessemer residents spent part of 1978 and 1979 seeking to get Marquez out of office because he was not supporting their position on various important issues. They were successful in getting Marquez out of office, but more importantly they displayed a new wave in Chicano thought. This new psychology, new ideology, has been forming and advancing within the Chicano community. This extension of the internal colonial model serves to explain or change the psychology, the worldview, of Chicanos: what is thought, what factors influence daily life, the breaking of oppressive barriers. It has been assumed that the internal colonial model's call for decolonization means that changes at the institutional level will affect individuals at the personal level. No doubt they will, to an extent, but this takes away from the individual Chicano the ability to think and act for herself/himself in her/his own way and in the community's interest. Change must come not only at various institutional levels. At a very personal level, the mind must be freed of traditional ways of thinking so that people can act differently. A decolonization of the way people think, what they value, how they conduct their lives is the next phase in community empowerment. Liberation begins with a thought. This thought, followed by action, is the root of the liberation force.

CIVIL DISCONTENT

Bessemer Chicanos in the late 1970s revealed a desire to act for themselves, to free themselves from opposing forces, and they took steps toward it; but things have not changed much. The forces at work against them 20 years ago were greater than they thought, and the struggle continues to this day. Not much has changed in Bessemer. The mill has downsized significantly. Because of this, in the 1980s Bessemer residents were in a severe economic and social depression. Now, in the 1990s, Chicanos feel they have tried to work within the system. They are still attempting a peaceful approach to solving the problems of discrimination in the United States; but for many this approach is much too slow.

Ideological development has been inconsistent; not all Chicanos developed in the same direction at the same time. Social forces have the power to create a homogenous nature, way of thinking and doing, in the group. The dominant society has been very successful, via education, the legal system, and other strategies in getting Chicanos to internalize the dominant social values of individuality, competition, upward mobility, and the profit motive. Most Chicanos now see themselves as superior to the environment. They move into overcrowded cities. They go to school. They use too much water. They pollute the air and earth. They kill one another. They beat up and rape women and children because of a hierarchical belief system.

Conquered people, people who do not enter a social system voluntarily, do not forget or give up culture easily. The Chicano struggle goes on because of this fact and because the communities continue. When their communities are destroyed, Chicanos lose the cultural battle. The same is true of language. In the 1980s, the English-only political push sought to destroy the use of Spanish. In some states, like New Mexico, activists easily defeated this measure. In other states the battle was much more difficult, and some lost.

In some places Chicanos are losing their communities. They are losing the effort to preserve the community's physical space, its morale. Communities are overcrowed, the earth is suffocated with plastics and toxic waste, clean air and water are being exhausted. In some regions the rich are very rich, and the very poor are on the street. The distance between the real and the ideal, between women and men, between heterosexuals and homosexuals are clearly obvious. Other communities have not "advanced" to this stage. They are vigilant, but few have noticed the war in their streets. Chicanos are very aware of this secret war. Those who have chosen to go to war have fought heroically in all arenas. Chicanas, especially, are very aware that women and children endure war, that war is a male endeavor, and that they are left to rear children by themselves when war kills and destroys men. The curtailment of war in their own country, the war on people of color in U.S. society, is essential in their eyes. Chicanos see and feel the civil discontent. They know that the responses to the Rodney King beating and the L.A. riots are an indication of what can happen in the back and front yards of raza, on the busy streets of this country. Germane to keeping the peace is social change, via the creation of social space and the elimination of the cycle of poverty.

REFERENCES

Barrera, Mario. 1979. *Race and Class in the Southwest*. Notre Dame: University of Notre Dame Press.

Blea, Irene I. 1988. *Toward a Chicano Social Science*. New York: Praeger, pp. 129, 146.

Cox, Oliver. 1970. *Caste, Class and Race*. New York: Modern Reader. Originally published in 1948.

Du Bois, W.E.B. 1967. *The Philadelphia Negro*. New York: Benjamin Blam.

Green, Rayna, and Frank W. Porter III. 1992. *Women in American Indian Society*. New York: Chelsea House Publisher, pp. 43–55.

Padilla, Genaro M. 1993. *My History, No Yours: The Formation of Mexican American Autobiography*. Madison: The University of Wisconsin Press.

Roco, Raymond A. 1976. "The Chicano in Social Sciences: Traditional Concepts, Myths and Images." *Aztlan: International Journal of Chicano Studies* (Spring). Los Angeles: Chicano Cultural Center.

U.S. Department of Commerce, Bureau of the Census. 1993. "We the American Hispanics," November, p. 5.

Vista. 1994. Vol. 9, no. 6 (February 9): 16.

One of the most powerful female symbols in Chicano culture is La Virgen de Guadalupe, a blending of indigenous and European culture.

9   Contemporary Issues

The primary task of this chapter is to outline current issues in Chicano communities. In addition to those already discussed, these issues include the life cycle, leisure time, environmental preservation, housing, the elderly. In the process of outlining some of these issues examples of inter- and intra-group relations are presented. Intergroup relations are defined as relations, interactions, among Chicanos. Intragroup relations describe interactions between Chicanos and other racial/ethnic groups. Thus, this chapter emphasizes the individual, how she/he relates to the issues, and how these issues impact the ways groups of people associate. A fundamental assumption is that one cannot understand the current community without understanding how it came to be the way it is. Contemporary issues are often symptoms of historical relationships. Urban leisure time, the small businesses in Chicano communities, the quality of life for youth, welfare recipients, and the unemployed are also explored in this chapter.

SOCIAL-HISTORICAL CONTEXT

An analysis of a community, whether it be in the 1970s or the 1990s, Chicano or non-Chicano, needs to examine why, when, how, and by whom it was founded. After this, emphasis is placed upon intragroup interactions. For example, Bessemer was founded in conjunction with the Bessemer Iron Works, which was established in February 1880, in Pueblo, Colorado. Bessemer was not part of Pueblo but a separate CF&I company town. The iron works, which later became the CF&I, bought land and literally built the town of Bessemer. Thus, Pueblo grew to be a city in bits and pieces. In the late 1800's, the real estate department of Bessemer Iron Works administered properties that were rented or leased by the company. These properties have now been incorporated into

Pueblo city proper and include buildings for public and private use. H. Lee Scamehorn (1966) notes that the iron works also controlled grazing land in the Arkansas, Cucharas, and Purgatory valleys. Large holdings of land prompted the CF&I to take an active role in developing irrigation facilities. Thus, the regional population very early grew dependent upon the company, and they continued to be dependent until the late 1980s when production slowed almost to a stopping point and the mill almost closed down. Today a company from Nebraska has purchased the mill, and Chicanos are working in cooperation with the several owners. The mill still has an overwhelming influence over the city.

In 1888, the iron works had organized the Bessemer Ditch Company. The company constructed a canal to transport water through the CF&I to CF&I agricultural lands in the Arkansas valley. That canal still exists today, and it runs through the heart of Bessemer, not far from the central business district, and forms the southernmost boundary of Bessemer. In the late 1970s the ditch was the center of much controversy. The water daily threatened persons in the community. Many Bessemer residents had drowned in the ditch. Two automobiles had gone through the chain link fence. One actually went into the water. People complained that the fencing along the ditch was not high enough, and it was only in the 1970s that fencing even existed. It was not uncommon to see Chicano children playing along the ditch because private property bordered the ditch.

Such long-lasting threats are not uncommon in poor Chicano communities. Just as it had done in years past, in the summer of 1979, the community addressed the issues of water seepage from the ditch into private homes and onto private property. Water seepage had caused uncalculable damage (Blea, 1991) to homes largely belonging to elderly Chicanos, a few Anglos, and a few African Americans. The citizens presented their grievances to the city council and explored alternative means of solving their problems. Property owners organized the Committee for Representative Government and chose to run their own candidate for city council. This effort is repeated day after day in Chicano communities throughout the nation.

On several occasions residents found that the CF&I was not working in their own interests. In 1879, miners of Mexican ancestry were first hired by the company for the mines in southern Colorado. Scamehorn (1966) writes that it is not certain if these workers were Mexicans from Mexico or Mexican Americans from New Mexico. There is some indication that indigenous Mexican American workers were hired first because they provided cheap labor. After this group of workers went out on strike, the company went to Monterey, Mexico, to recruit new, exploitable labor. Later African Americans, Italians, and Austrians were brought to break one another's strikes in 1884 and 1885. Today, this ethnic composition is highly reflected in Bessemer and other parts of Pueblo. There can still be found several African Americans, many elderly Italians, and a few Serbs and other Slovenians in Bessemer. African Americans are not found in high numbers in other parts of the city. Italians and Slovenians have experienced much more upward mobility. The white Europeans have moved out of Bessemer and Chicanos dominate, in numbers only. In 1978–1979, they had no real power. Only a few younger members of this population have moved out. Various seniors in the community reported that for many years English was the second language of Bessemer. It was only used outside of the family and circle of friends.

The CF&I established the Sociological Department on July 25, 1901, when Dr. Richard Warner Corwin was given general charge of it (Scamehorn, 1966). The department was to concern itself with the community: health, education, housing, sanitation, recreation. Its manifest objective was to dispense information and to create an environment that would make workers desirous of doing the best they could for themselves and their employer. Scamehorn suggests that the department may have been prompted by a coal miners strike and the Colorado general assembly's criticism of CF&I labor policies. CF&I mining towns were for the most part neglected and unattractive, offering few community services.

The department recognized that workers came from different ethnic backgrounds and that it needed to impose a common culture. It provided for the workers and their families a host of services, including education, housing, police and fire protection, plus leisure activities. It was profitable to "Americanize" workers. Corwin assumed that children of workers would become future CF&I employees, or wives of employees, and should acquire skills required for these roles. One of these skills was education in the English language. In the summer of 1901, the Sociological Department launched five programs in the fields of education, social training, industrial training, housing, and communications. The programs were age stratified: for children, mothers, homemakers, working adults, and the elderly. The department conducted courses for women in domestic science, with instruction in food preparation, sewing, and housekeeping. Corwin believed it was difficult to change the values and ways of mature persons, so he concentrated his efforts upon the children. Intensive kindergarten programs were created, as were homes for teachers, which also served as headquarters for social workers. The furnishings in these homes were deliberately selected to serve as examples to local homemakers of what could be accomplished, at modest costs, in their own homes. The idea was to have women return home and prompt their husbands to work to make money so that they could have such furnishings.

The CF&I was the largest landowner and taxpayer in southern Colorado, and it made demands on other parts of the city with respect to buildings, teacher competency, and textbooks. Corwin influenced the state superintendent of public instruction to supply uniform courses throughout the mining camps. This allowed children to move from one camp to another without disturbing their education. Night courses offered instruction in speaking, reading, and writing English to adults. For a charge of $1.00 per month students could also learn geography and history. Scamehorn rationalizes these programs on the grounds that in 1901 there were 32 nationalities and 27 different languages, excluding dialects, in the mining camps. Few could read or write in any language.

The Sociological Department moved into other areas. The Industrial Home located on East Abriendo Avenue in Bessemer offered employment to men who had been permanently injured in the mill or in the mines. It also provided employment to widows and children of deceased workers. At this home, they manufactured mattresses, brooms, hammocks, furniture, rugs, carpets, lace, and other products in demand in the local communities.

Today, in Bessemer there are are still numerous bars and a few liquor stores. They are frequently the social centers for men and certain kinds of women. The presence of the bars attests to Scamehorn's contention that saloons also flourished as social centers in mining towns. To discourage patronage of local bars, the company established recreational halls that did not permit liquor. Because gambling was a questionable activity, it was strictly regulated. In the camps, bootlegging was common. One of the Bessemer informants related that many Bessemer men were injured and died from "bad booze." Another experiment to control drinking was the close supervision of bars by company employees. Drinks were served under well-defined regulations. Those bar owners who did not comply 'would have their bars closed and would be removed from the community. Drinking regulations were printed in English, German, and Italian. Some interesting questions arise, for instance, does the absence of Spanish signs mean that Mexican American workers were not allowed in the bars? There is no answer to this in the Scamehorn account. The entire thrust of this antidrinking campaign, however, was to keep workers sober so they could work. The recreation halls served other functions, as classrooms and housing circulating libraries, art collections, lectures, stereopticon shows, concerts, plays, and dances.

The Minnequa Town Company, a subsidiary directed by Dr. Corwin, built dwellings and other structures for the corporation in Bessemer. Scamehorn relates that in the early history of Bessemer, housing was mixed and varied in quality. It included neat, practical frame units, log cabins, adobes, dugouts, and shacks. Unlike other mining towns, in Bessemer houses were readily available. In the late 1970s Bessemer housing was not controlled by the CF&I, but it was still highly influenced by it. It was crowded and uneven in development. In the mid 1990s a parking lot and a few CF&I buildings east of it served as reminders that the company store and the recreation center once stood there.

INTER- AND INTRA-GROUP RELATIONS

Several factors affecting inter- and intra-group relations have been discussed. One element not yet focused upon is the media, as well as its historical development in Chicano communities. Radio, T.V., newspapers, and magazines are important because they document and communicate information that can affect how people behave. In each community it is important to assess who controls the media, who defines it. The power of the media is rooted in how it is related to other social institutions, how it permeates the social structure, and how it can be used for social control. In Bessemer, from 1901 to 1904, the Sociological Department published a company newspaper entitled *The Camp and Plant*. A subscription cost $1.00 a year, and most employees read it. *The Camp and Plant* was also used by the the Medical Department, which was also run by Dr. Corwin. The Sociological Department continued to pursue its goals until 1915, when the famous Ludlow Massacre resulted in the deaths of Chicanos and other ethnic workers when they went on strike. This massacre critically disrupted the CF&I, and John D. Rockefeller adopted the Industrial Representation Plan as a means of restoring harmony.

Newspaper articles appeared in German, Italian, Spanish, and Slavonic. Most of these languages are now rarely spoken in Bessemer, although Spanish is still widely used. In the 1980s most Spanish-speaking communities were locked into legislative battles over English as the official language. This English-only effort was seen as oppressive, taking away their language, killing their culture, and making Chicanos dependent on English.

Conversations with contemporary workers and historical accounts of CF&I history quickly reveal some basic antagonisms. One of them was between workers and CF&I officials. This antagonism was also present in the community where the two groups lived. In the 1970s Chicanos were refusing foreman positions because if they accepted them, they would have to protect the interests of the company and would be alienated from their fellow workers. Workers often harassed foremen and saw them as the enemy. In the late 1970s Chicano workers were well acquainted with racism, but had only begun to identify sexism. Lawsuits by workers had not only been directed against the mill owners but also against the union representatives, whom the workers saw as being in close alliance with the company. What happened to Chicanos in the steel industry and in other industrial complexes was very important because these industries were the last vestiges of industrialization in the United States. The United States was moving into a postindustrial era of high technology. It affected Bessemer residents negatively, as the mill began to use advanced technology and lay off workers.

ECONOMIC DEVELOPMENT

Even though they experienced discrimination on the job, most Chicanos did not file discrimination complaints and law suits. The antidiscrimination body of legislation was put in place to protect them. In the late 1970s, the CF&I had been charged by the Bessemer residents with discrimination, issuing economic threats, and partial responsibility for flooding poor people's basements. Residents were most upset because decisions that affected them were being made by people who did not live in their community. This issue is very much alive today in communities around the United States. In Bessemer, many people did not like the alley paving program. They liked seeing raw earth; they enjoyed walking on the ground; they felt connected to it. A layer of asphalt would place a barrier between them and Mother Earth. The policy was seen as culturally destructive by some, but most did not know why they didn't want the alleys paved. They only knew that they did not like it.

In documenting the lives of Chicanos, the researcher should keep in mind the public and the private face, two distinct ways of presenting one's self. Lives that are very interesting and more true to the nature of the community can be found in people's back yards. In many cases there appears to be a contradiction between the front and back yards. Most often, there is a public face represented in the front yard, and a more relaxed, private face represented in the back yard. Yards are the exterior, the boundary, the shell of the space that is lived in. Front yards are more often better kept than back yards. In the back yards of the 1970s women hung clothes, dried chilies and dried wool, which they had washed from pillows and mattresses. In the back yards men repaired automobiles, stored tools, and prepared for fishing and hunting trips. Very few Chicanos barbecued. Instead, they played with their children and grandchildren. Children played with one another, and neighbors visited. This is also where most gardens of squash, tomatoes, zucchini, chili, and beans were planted. Back yards were also used to keep large dogs, wrecked automobiles, and children's toys. Today, the back yards and alleys can be dangerous. They are the prime targets of thieves and drug addicts and are places for gang hangouts. A lack of economic development has caused residents in some communities to lock themselves and their children indoors. Not only are back yards, alleys, and vacant lots dangerous, the front yard is no longer as well maintained because it can mark a house as more affluent, making it subject to breaking and entry. The front yard and the front room are also the targets for drive by shootings.

In the mid 1970s, Spanish-surnamed females and males, married and unmarried, were frequently locked into lower-paying, more hazardous jobs. Mostly non-Spanish surnamed workers were promoted to supervisory positions, but Spanish surnamed workers incurred fewer injuries and experienced fewer on-the-job deaths per year (Blea, 1991). More research is required in order to compare the 1970s with the mid-1990s. Through the 1970s Chicano workers and their families adhered to the working-class work ethic, and some even earned middle-class incomes. They knew they had what was necessary to "succeed," to be worthwhile citizens in the United States, but they were still discriminated against. In the 1980s some were deceived by the prosperous declaration of "The Decade of the Hispanic." In the mid-1990s Chicanos are still not accorded the status, power, and prestige afforded to Anglo Americans. In the mid 1990s gainfully employed Chicanos still have a sense of raza apart from the mainstream, of being Chicano or Mexican American, a sense of identification with other Latinos. This identification is frequently tested when there is conflict between the newly arrived immigrant and the long-term resident. This happens because members of the Chicano population are not too long removed from poverty and they do not want to be reflected upon negatively by the condition of the immigrant groups. Inter-group conflict sometimes happens because the raza forget that the immigrants are also raza, and they have inherited the victimization, the legacy, of the colonial experience.

Chicanos spend their money where they live, and they tend to live where they work. Some live in suburban areas, but most live in cities. Those living in the suburbs are an interesting group and are in need of study. Those in barrios are the best studied. Even though, nationally, most Chicano small businesspersons are in food services, many are not. Small businesses include record stores, video stores, very small pharmacies, grocery stores, furniture shops, auto body shops, flower shops, and used or second-hand stores. Women are not highly represented in the small business world, although many operate beauty shops. Women tend to work in automated laundries, in bakeries, in other small businesses like tortilla factories, and as seamstresses.

THE DISENFRANCHISED

The economic structure of most Chicano communities includes a substantial segment of the population that exists on state and federally funded programs. Ranking high in this Bessemer population were single mothers, young children, and senior citizens and their dependents. This population tended to derive their income from "welfare" checks, purchase food with food stamps, pay for medical services with medicaid or medicare, get free school lunches, and generally have little or no money to spend on quality housing, leisure activities, clothing, other nonfood items, and transportation. In the late 1970s, jobs were scarce, and many had given up looking for work.

David offers an example of the problems encountered by Bessemer young men. For one year I watched David experience the difficulties of seeking employment: going from one "manpower," federally funded, position to another, standing in line, getting laid off, and waiting. David's parents were originally from Mexico. He was born and had grown up in Bessemer. He confided that he was depressed and just did not feel good. He blamed his "bad luck" on his war experience in Vietnam. He was more fortunate than other men his age; he had graduated from high school and "from time to time" had attended the university on his G.I. benefits in an attempt to get some of the skills the war had denied him. There were times when David felt better, but he more frequently felt a deep sense of failure because of lack of employment and what is known as the delayed depressive reaction syndrome to the Vietnam experience.

There were many chronically unemployed young men in Bessemer. Some were more fortunate than David because they had not been to Vietnam. After meeting David in 1979 I began to think about the social factors that characterize the male gender role. Focus at the time was on how young men in the Chicano communities were more highly victimized by racism, not sexism. Most, but not all, had internalized feelings of failure, and some had recognized that success for males in U.S. society is clearly linked to earning capacity. That discrimination had blocked this avenue to "success" was hardly recognized. The Vietnam experience exacerbated this. The young men who were Vietnam veterans in the late 1970s are now 45- and 50-year-old men. Many outlived the massive suicides, incarcer-

ations, drug and alcohol addiction of Vietnam veterans; but, intentionally or unintentionally, so many were self-destructive. These Chicano young men were
generally working class or poor men in the 1960s when they went to war at age 18
or 19 and their psycho-sexual development was interrupted. When they came
home, they returned to poverty, unemployment, continued discrimination, and
a loud protest against the war. While they were in Vietnam, or upon their return,
they gained race consciousness and some even joined the massive protests. The
war split the community into those who claimed to be more patriotic and those
who appeared to be less. This split exists today in Bessemer, in San Antonio, in
Denver, in Los Angeles, wherever large populations of Chicanos are encountered. In the rural areas patriotism is sometimes higher due to the lack of a critical voice. Unemployment and poverty are also higher.

Gunnar Myrdal (1944) lent insight into poverty in the early 1940s. He established that discrimination set into motion a domino effect, resulting in low education, low economic power, low health status, and low political power. Few
American sociologists paid attention to the German immigrant's focus on black
America. African American and Chicano scholars revived and expanded upon
Myrdal's work in the 1960s. In the 1990s the cycle of poverty is well established
in American academia.

In order to avoid this cycle, Chicanos and other Americans know that it now
takes two persons working full time to support a family. Those who cannot
"make it" suffer from a deep sense of failure, psychological and sometimes spiritual hardship. "Making it" has come to mean being able to provide the essen-
tials for a healthy life. This is different from the late 1970s when "making it"
meant having money to engage in leisure activity.

EXPLORING THE LIFE CYCLE

The life cycle is outlined as beginning with the elderly. Elders are still important in Chicano/Latino culture. With age comes status; but in order to more fully
explore the Chicano life cycle, three areas need more research. They include the
Chicano or Latino elderly, male gender roles, and how people spend leisure
time. Life in Bessemer is different now from what it was in the 1970s. Almost 30
years ago, Sundays in Bessemer were generally slower days. Today, they are busy
days with individuals trying frantically to meet social obligations to family and
friends and shopping for groceries and other necessities. In 1994, the Chavezes
complain of loneliness because one of their sons (a Pentecostal minister) died in
an automobile accident. Their daughters, daughters-in-law, and two other sons
are working: one son in Denver and another at the nearby steel mill. They
missed the family life of the 1970s. The grandchildren are grown and busy with
their friends. In the 1970s Friday and Saturday evenings were extremely busy
because of the high number of bars and because a major nightclub existed in
Bessemer. The nightclub has burned down and the bars are full of Mexican immigrants. The Chavezes no longer go to dances and dislike the recent immi-

grants. There is less teenage "cruising" in cars, and gasoline is plentiful, thus lines at the gas pumps are much shorter. Children no longer play on the sidewalks because parents fear kidnapping and drive by shootings. In the 1970s traffic of both people and vehicles began about 8:00 P.M. and did not end until well after 2:00 A.M. Bessemer is quieter now. Few Mexican restaurants stay open "after hours" to feed the loud, hungry crowds who had generally been happy from drinking. Mexican Americans fear violence and simply do not want to associate with recent immigrants and undocumented workers. In the late 1970s, during these Friday and Saturday night hours, the local "wino" who "mooched" drinks and respectable married couples could both be out for an evening of entertainment at the same place. "Mooching" is no longer tolerated, and fewer married couples go out.

Nationally known Chicano artists who once made personal appearances in area nightclubs now play at the arts center, and single heterosexual persons look for partners at a nightclub across town. Homosexuals are taboo in Bessemer, and it is difficult to get information on this segment of the population. As in the late 1970's, many women live alone with children. Old women and men are seen on the streets, but only during the daylight hours. Gangs are talked about in Bessemer, but Bessemer is luckier than other parts of the city for there are none. In the 1970s violence was in the form of domestic violence and barroom fights. Today, Bessemer is plagued by the same things that plague larger cities. In the 1970s, the police were well known and generally kept order. People no longer know the police, and they are generally disliked and distrusted. All in all, Bessemer has changed. Low riders are no longer seen on the streets. Mexican Americans shop by day but turn the streets over to recent Mexican immigrants at night. Mexican American women who date immigrant men are considered cheap, and the shared space is divided.

The lack of facilities for youth is still an issue in Bessemer. While doing my initial study I met 13-year-old Sofie, who was part Puerto Rican and part Mexican American. Her Mexican American mother had reared her and a son by herself. Today, Sofie is a divorced mother of two. She married one of the boys from Los Dukes, a group that was trying to be a gang in the 1970s. Her ex-husband is now in prison. Sofie's friends reported that they were occasionally questioned about Sofie's heritage because she looked different. Her children resemble their Mexican American father. On two or three occasions Sofie and her friends had physically fought with other teenagers because of name calling that involved racial slurs directed at Sofie. Sofie still carries the scars of this. Her father lived in Puerto Rico, and Sofie stirred up a great deal of interest when her father took her to Puerto Rico, to visit during a Christmas vacation almost 30 years ago. The father sometimes sent money or gifts, and Sofie reported that he also treated her four-year-old brother, who was not his son, very well. Sofie rarely hears from her father today. Her brother Carlos's father is an undocumented worker who had returned to Mexico, and he has not been heard from since Carlos was a year old. Sofie and I kept track of how she spent her time. Below is a typical day.

June 30, Saturday

10:30	Got up and fixed the bed
11:00	Set up the sweeper
11:30	Watched T.V.
12:30	Listened to the radio
12:30	Cleaned house
1:30	Talked on the phone
2:30	Went to the park
4:00	Went to play pool
5:30	Watched T.V.
7:00	Went to the park
9:00	Baby-sat (while mother socialized in the Bessemer bars and nightclubs)

Often Bessemer youth, like Sofie, were left unsupervised and to their own devices in seeking recreation. In the 1970s, and now, there was/is no comprehensive recreation center in the area, and single parent households are generally depressed. Young women like Sofie generally marry young, have two or three children, and get divorced at least twice. Like Sofie they sometimes "end up" on welfare, but they survive. Sofie was intelligent and creative as a youth. She got good grades in school and read extensively. Her mother said she was proud of her and verbally encouraged her. Yet the mother behaved in ways that did not role model what she wanted for her daughter. More research needs to be done on how young women like Sofie break the welfare cycle, go to the university, and are gainfully employed. Sofie is characteristic of those in the Chicano community who are paraprofessionals and professionals and are willing to assist others out of poverty, but not always out of the barrio.

ENVIRONMENTAL ISSUES

Native Americans and raza were the first environmentalists. Raza learned much from indigenous cultures and shared some of their Moorish irrigation knowledge with native people. Together, their impact upon the land was minimal. Today communities worry about toxic waste from scientific experiments, chemical production, and human consumption. Generally, dump sites are rural issues, but they are also urban issues and coupled with air and noise pollution they show a drastic need for health services. Both in the city and in the rural areas there is a need for transportation. Those outside the rural areas wonder why Mexican Americans and Indians live in poor houses and have ill health but drive expensive pickup trucks. Rural people need good transportation and sacrifice to get it because they drive long distances to work, to the doctor, to school, and for groceries. Cities are overcrowded, few have reliable transportation, and there is a need for public transportation in areas not already serviced by it. Other environmental issues have to do with cultural maintenance, cultural destruction, and appropriation by Anglos. This is most evident in traditionally Mexican American cities like Santa Fe, New Mexico, where East and West Coast Anglos purchase land and obstruct scenic views, disrespect native people, change religious practices, and raise prices. Just having to look at Anglos sickens some Chicanos in Santa Fe.

Is this Chicano racism? Chicano reasons for the dislike of Anglos are not based upon appearance, or national background. They occur because of Anglo appropriation of resources, Anglo social and environmental impact, and what is perceived as general negative behavior and disrespect for Chicano culture. One Santa Fe resident said it plainly, "They ruined where they lived and now want to come here where they will ruin where we have lived for centuries." Anglos are perceived as not valuing things not in the Anglo interests (generally, producing a profit). Anglos are seen to possess an instant culture, where they discard things and people, declare things illegal and ridicule what they do not understand.

In Bessemer, for example, some residents felt the ditch was no longer in the Anglo-controlled CF&I interest, thus it was abandoned, and the residents had to fix the damage it was causing. Research on the claim revealed that, indeed, the ditch was no longer essential to the CF&I and that private farmers, living in the nearby Arkansas Valley, relied on the ditch for irrigation water in the summer. In the summer it ran full and basements in the city got flooded, mosquitoes flocked to the area, and life was generally miserable. During the winter months, water was not needed in such high quantities, the water level was lower, basements did not get flooded, and cold weather kept the mosquitoes away. The solution to the problem, for the Anglo-controlled city council, was to wait for the summer to pass.

Added to this was the issue of air pollution. Driving toward the city of Pueblo after crossing hundreds of miles of open plains or descending from the Sangre de Cristo Mountains under clear blue skies, the frightening sight of air tinted reddish brown or grey was more than unsightly. Pueblo residents were suspicious of what was in the air. They blamed the CF&I for polluting the air, and, indeed, it was the culprit. Both city and CF&I officials maintained that Pueblo air was among the purest in the state. A report of unknown origin blamed the dry prairie and residents' unpaved alleys for dust in the air. In 1979, after years of political volleying, CF&I pollution controls were the strongest in the nation. The CF&I contended that though the corporation was probably the state's largest single consumer of energy resources, it had managed to decrease its use of fuel oil by 89 percent. It dropped its consumption of natural gas by 50 percent and increased consumption of coal-derived electricity by 20 to 25 percent. Although the CF&I claimed it only made about 1.5 percent of all U.S. steel, it was still a monster in the state of Colorado (Blea, 1991).

It was sad that most Bessemer males who worked in the mill in the 1970s hated their jobs, but when it slowed, then closed, down they were severely distraught. The plant's union, the city officials, and other community pressures were helpless in stopping the devastating slowdown and final closure. Chicano

dependency had fostered a schizophrenic relationship with the physical structure and the people who controlled it. During and after the massive slowdown
and final closure, life in Bessemer became depressed. Not only was there economic depression, but the people themselves were depressed, although few left
Bessemer. In 1994, interviews with Organ Steel (CF&I's successor) workers reveal that, for the most part, the male workers do not like their jobs and do not
want their sons to work there.

Cultural control can be linked to the control of the environment. A return to
the 1978–1979 Bessemer study will demonstrate that even then Chicano communities were toxic waste dumps. Smoke and fumes emanated from the CF&I
and the interstate highway that separated the mill from the community. Until the
late 1960s small black- and rust-colored particles were carried in the air, covering
rooftops, windows, trees, grass, and the laundry the women hung on clotheslines
in the neighborhood. An unusually foul odor, which people said came from the
coke plant, enveloped everything when it was discharged. Most homes were of
wood frame and stucco construction; they were tinted with this smell and dust.
There were a few brick homes and fewer adobes, which were less dusty.

Most Bessemer homes had front porches that were used heavily in the summer evenings as a means of escaping the 100 degree heat, which got trapped in
the house. Evenings on the porch led to much conversation and knowledge
about the neighbors. Most homes had front yard lawns and a few had back yard
lawns. In the summer lawns were trimmed with flowers: marigolds, petunias,
zinnias. Other full-sun flowers, such as hollyhocks, brightened up some very dis-
mal surroundings. There were also ceramic swans and ducks in people's yards.
In a display of Catholicism, statues of the Virgin Mary, encased in ceramic tubs
buried halfway in the ground, were evident.

In the summer of 1978, the arches over the tubs holding the Virgin Mary
were decorated with flowers. Candles were placed before the "Blessed Virgin."
The Virgin Mary is of special significance to the Spanish-speaking people of the
Southwest. "Nuestra Senora de Guadalupe," who is an Indian version of the bib-
lical Mary, is the patron saint of Mexico. In the 1990s, the image of la Virgin de
Guadalupe appeared on many home altars and a few murals on the walls of area
residents. Her image appeared on calendars, in frames on walls, and as images
on low riders. Unlike the Mexican Virgin de Guadalupe, the Bessemer outdoor
statues were clothed in blue and lacked the dark skin coloring of the Guadalupe
Virgin Mary. This observation is important because there are two kinds of Spanish-speaking populations living in Bessemer: recent immigrants of Mexican origin and old New Mexican families. The New Mexicans tended to recognize the
more European deity, the Mexicans the Guadalupe. A 1994 visit to Bessemer
revealed that upon exiting Interstate 25 onto Evans Avenue I encountered the
same, but now faded, Virgin Mary that was there in 1978. In 1978, the virgin had
already been in the same place for 12 years.

It is painful for Chicanos to see the environment destroyed. Respect for
Mother Earth is an element of their indigenous culture. They are related to the

earth, the sky, the flowers, the trees, the fish, the water in the rivers, the coyote in the foothills, the birds, the pigeons, the squirrels. In the very recent past, they also recognized that they were related to one another as human beings. Racism, sexism, industrialization, and urbanization have severely threatened the way they live; and some are even so full of frustration and self-hate that they hurt their own people and their own environment.

REFERENCES

Blea, Irene I. 1991. *Bessemer: A Sociological Perspective of A Chicano Barrio*. New York: AMS Press.

Myrdal, Gunnar. 1944. *American Dilemma*. New York: Pantheon.

Scamehorn, H. Lee. 1966. *Pioneer Steelmakers in the West*. Boulder: Pruett Publishing Company.

Rural senior gentleman wearing a straw hat in the city.

10   Healing a Nation

This chapter contends that the nation must heal itself from the wounds caused by historical violence of discrimination because the social costs are too high. The chapter gives examples of how to promote healing and how to link the social sciences to social activism via theoretical approaches and activities in the community that can bridge differences and stop the social conflict. Chicanos and other ethnic/racial people have a leading role in this healing because most of them have been the victims, and because so many of them have developed coping mechanisms that can strengthen both the social sciences and the society. This healing, of course, requires that the dominant culture recognize that wrongs have been committed and that people of color have knowledge built upon ancient civilizations in addition to skills gained from having endured discrimination. In short, they have learned to survive and have something to teach. Atonement, forgiveness, and reinforcement play a role here; as does mutual honor, respect, and apology. This chapter is but the first step in plotting a journey that changes attitude and behavior. It is a long journey, pitted by obstacles, but not impossible.

ENCOUNTERING CONTRADICTIONS AND HISTORICAL TRAUMA

It did not take Chicano activists long to find out that to control knowledge is to control people and information, and that there is a large discrepancy between the ideal and real social conditions in this country, which promises freedom and justice for all. Thus, Chicanos lack trust in those who symbolize this promise; they have come to fear injustice. Perhaps the biggest Chicano and Chicana fear is having to give up or lose the fragile hold they have on their own culture. Put simply, they no longer want to be exploited by dominant Americans, and they do not want to be absorbed by their values. In addition, they want the inconsistent standards for social participation based on ethnicity, race, or color, especially women of color, to be corrected. They do not want to have individualistic, profit-oriented, competitive dominant American values imposed on their communal way of life. They also do not want talented Chicanos with resources to be lost to the Chicano community and to their families. Perhaps Anglos fear that if people of color come into power, then they will treat Anglos the way Anglos have treated people of color. Perhaps, if racism ends, Anglos fear they will lose their privileged position in the society that values white skin color. Perhaps Anglos fear that the bases upon which their society rests will be revealed as lies and will crumble. From a Chicano perspective, the biggest hope is that their extended community will become socially stable and that discrimination against them will end.

Dominant Americans must understand that America promised freedom and justice for all, and that people of color believe in this premise and expect it. They have tried to Americanize, to work within the system, and it has not delivered what it promised. From their perspective the system is rigged against them. Basically, they feel they have kept their share of the bargain and dominant American culture, Anglo controlled, has not delivered on its share. Because both side have retreated into a world that is hostile, Chicanos and other people of color have been left angry, empty, lost, fearful, or confused. Anger is the most threatening. It costs lives. Sometimes people lash out at the oppressor, causing individuals, and entire groups, to become disoriented, depressed, self-destructive, without cultural reference, and without harmony or peace.

Although the general population of the United States did not note it, the nation was at war in 1992 when riots broke out in south central Los Angeles over the court ruling on the beating of African American Rodney King by white police officers. But, the entire nation paid attention to what they believed was self-destruction as blacks, Asians, and Latinos looted, robbed, and beat up others. Los Angeles, and its metropolitan area, is often the pulse of this country; and here Reginald Denny, an Anglo truck driver, was violently beaten by African American young men. Modern technology is such that the beating, like that of black Rodney King, was shown on national television.

The 19 million people of the Los Angeles region represent almost every country. Chicanos/Latinos and African Americans are a major part of it. The coloring of America is a real phenomenon, one that cities are contending with daily. During the riots people were shocked and could hardly believe what the country had come to. After the riots, people were fearful. They conducted themselves cautiously or hid in fear; and they mourned their state of inhumanity. What most failed to note was that the incident was/is important because it symbolized race relations in the nation.

To note that the United States is a violent culture has become a common cliche. Competition is a well-defined dominant American cultural attribute. People of color have become frustrated attempting to compete in a game that is biased against them by unwritten rules. This frustration, and the consequences of not succeeding, has bred violence. Violence and competition are most apparent in riots, but they are also apparent in how people of color are forced to think and act in a culturally inconsistent manner to the dominant hierarchical social order in order to survive. This is not their natural way of acting and thinking. Yet they have tolerated it, have given the system a chance to give them a chance, but the chance has not come for entire groups. It is the group that counts, not the individual.

The violence, competition, and individualism of the dominant culture is apparent in everything to people of color. It is apparent in the dichotomies and in the racist language Chicanos have learned to use: "up town, down town," "lowest man on the totem pole," "Mexican standoff." It is apparent in how academic progress is graded from A to F; first grade, second grade; K through 12 versus higher education; girls' bathroom, boys' bathroom. Entire groups of Anglos have not learned to speak Spanish, or any other language. Most are perceived as having little or no respect for people of different cultures, for the elderly, and for human life beyond their own. If they had, there would be no nursing homes. There would be home health care for the elderly. If the society valued women, antidiscrimination laws and domestic violence laws would be enforced. If the society valued the environment, there would be strict enforcement of environmental protection laws and a sense of a connectedness of the land, the air, the water, the plants. If Americans were equal, there would not be status cars, status neighborhoods, "old heaps," "clunkers," reservations, ghettos, and barrios. There would be no such thing as historical trauma.

Historical trauma is physical or emotional damage due to prolonged periods of abuse. Social abuse of people of color has been documented by scholars of ethnic studies and others. The fact that it exists is evident in that there actually exist legislation and policies that prevent discrimination. In the Chicano perspective, these pieces of legislation and policies have rarely been enforced. In fact, other legislation and policy are seen as preventing the United States from healing the injustices of discrimination. It impacts populations of color by robbing them of opportunity, thus maintaining them in subordinate conditions. On reservations, in ghettos, in barrios, and in other communities people of color are governed by laws created by Anglos, favoring Anglo culture.

Sometimes those in control formulate laws and policies that face one disempowered population against another. An example of this is funding of the arts and education, where the applicant develops a proposal and competes with other people of color. Legislation includes health laws that can accuse curanderas of practicing medicine without a license. There is legislation that governs what service providers are allowed to charge consumers, but people of color are charged more. In the case of death, for example, certain laws and policies govern how people are treated while receiving health treatment and how they are buried. While in the hospital, the patient may not be allowed to drink certain *remedios*, tea remedies, simply because the tea is not understood as a part of the patient's culturally biased diet. Healing rituals are not allowed, and regulations about visiting may prevent the extended family from visiting the patient, thereby slowing down the healing process due to lack of emotional support. Only a few health practitioners are beginning to realize that healing combines medical traditions at the physical, emotional, and spiritual levels. Even in death the law, the cost, and funeral parlor rules govern how the body is displayed, when it may be viewed, where it may be viewed, how mourners are received, and how the body is disposed of. Policies and laws, plus the cost of moving the body, do not allow for three-day or overnight vigils in the home.

Historical trauma is simply the contention that people have been treated in exclusionary and demeaning manners for a very long time. In its most severe manifestation it renders the wounded unable to thrive in her/his society. To a lesser degree it impacts the victim's self-esteem. It manifests as bad health, low education, a lack of political power, and higher rates of incarceration. These manifestations validate the Anglo culture as the favorable, true, correct culture and allows privilege and status to those who conform, in behavior and body type, by subjecting them to less discrimination. This elevates discriminatory practices into the ongoing institutional and cultural mechanism. When viewed from the outside, the Chicano may appear to suffer from loss of self-concept and self-esteem, but when viewed from the inside, Chicanos are seen to be highly motivated to protect their culture. This motivation incorporates high self-esteem and a concept of self that connotes value, and dominant Americans need to learn to respect this.

As has been discussed in chapter 8, discrimination begins at the cognitive level with misconceptions. This can be best understood in the analysis of Frantz Fanon (1963) and Albert Memmi (1965). The dominant group sets itself up as the most worthy group and presents evidence of their worthiness. They have the power to contrive or bend this evidence in their favor because they possess control of the institutions that present the evidence. The powerless adopt the ruling elite's conceptions about themselves and even their ideology to varying degrees. Some of the oppressed may come to believe they are too powerless to do anything about their condition. This perceptions shapes a predisposition to act in certain ways, to behave according to social prescription. It is through peoples acting on lies and misconceived perceptions that racism takes place. Laws, policies, and regulations help cement the social organization into place.

This process creates distrust not only on behalf of the victim but the perpetrators also live in a state of distrust. They fear revolt from the oppressed. The fear is compounded with the knowledge that what has happened to the oppressed can happen to them. Thus, traumatization is bad for the victim as well as the victimizer. In the case of discrimination, the racist, the sexist, and the homophobic are also sick. They cause harm not only to their victims but also to other members of the victims' racial/ethnic group and to the general society by robbing it of groups of individuals who could have made generous contributions to education, science, technology, and art.

Communities need to openly discuss the costs of discrimination. Persons with the ability to do this are already at the forefront of the discussions on drugs, homelessness, graffiti. They can assist a community in healing itself from discrimination if there is not a ferocious power struggle. They can determine where dialogues will take place, when, who will speaks first, who will have the last word. The power to impact decisions at this level is mostly illusionary. Those who believe that individuals possess real power often do not participate in a system that is oppressive to themselves and to others. Their current justification for power struggles is based on the belief that at least they have more resources than others. The key word here is "least." The society is least served by this mentality.

Discrimination can also create antagonisms as well as ambivalence. There is an ambivalence and an antagonism by some Chicanos toward life outside the barrio and of finding love or friendships with those who are not Chicanos. Many Bessemer residents felt that the Anglo way of life was "no good," "cold," and "impersonal." Antagonisms toward Anglos were encountered for no other reason than that they were Anglos. There was frequent antagonism to anything that was considered middle class, therefore Anglo. Sometimes these antagonisms were toward Chicanos who had adopted lifestyles that were middle class or *agrindado*, Angloized. This intolerance toward the Anglo and Anglo ways was in contrast to a tolerance to crowded conditions and things Anglos would think intolerable, even deviant.

There were Chicanos who were functioning very well outside the barrio but were still linked to it by work with its population. Some of these included two university professors who lived in a middle-income, mostly Anglo, area. They had combined higher education and the knowledge of local history and contemporary conditions in an effort to assist others in bettering their life chances and to promote social change. These Chicano professionals were at the forefront of change in the barrio, and in Pueblo as a whole. Theoretically, it could be said they had an intellectual understanding of the forces at work and sought to link theory to practice.

Also able to link theory to practice are the women, especially Chicanas. As women, they bring another perspective to the above area of discussion in that they have had a slightly different experience. Some differences between women and men, among human beings, complement, even enrich, life; but artificial, man-made, differences complicate it and produce unnecessary tensions and strife. Most Anglo men and women have taken advantage of privileges falsely accorded them by virtue of their skin color. In the process they have negated their responsibility to their community, to their society. Anglos, Chicanas, and Chicanos have a responsibility to make the life cycle less stressful.

Here the role of women can be particularly helpful. Most women have assumed the caretaker responsibility for themselves and for their men. Thus, women can play a big role in helping society heal from male dominance, sexism, and racism. Caretaking for contemporary women no long is limited to child rearing. They now bring home a major part of the family paycheck. On the job it means guarding against racism, sexism, and class discrimination and taking responsibility for sexuality and child rearing. It means the teaching of morals, values, and ethics not only at home, but outside and at the work place. It means tending a personal, emotional, physical, and spiritual life for themselves and for those around them. The truth is that because of changes in society, men have inherited, or at least have to share in, some of the work that women once did.

RECOGNIZING THE PROBLEM

It must be recognized that the struggles to link theory to practice in the area of discrimination have resulted in minimal social change. The issues today are the ones that existed in the 1960s. Those issues have been outlined in the previous chapters and focus upon living conditions, the criminal justice system, economics, education, politics, health, and spirituality. Anglo Americans, as a population, need to recognize that, indeed, Americans of color have also made outstanding contributions to America. Both have to weave these contributions into the fabric of mainstream culture.

There was a beginning in this direction when the Martin Luther King, Jr., holiday was established. There was much resistance to this. One of the major television stations noted Cesar Chavez among America's most noted persons who died in 1993. My suggestions, however, go beyond this, beyond having September dedicated as National Hispanic Heritage Month. The goal is to do away with these special designations. Various cultures will be studied in school, citizens should be able to speak two or more languages fluently.

It is not enough to note the special contributions of a group. The suffering of the group must be presented in schools and other public programming. This way there is no denial of hardship and pain. The suffering must be noted so that negative experiences will not be repeated. Noting the suffering validates the fact that it happened. It legitimizes the anger, the resistance, and makes it real to those who did not endure any pain. Much validation is needed in order to get Chicanos and other people of color to regain trust in the social institutions and conceive of a social space that does not keep them physically, socially, and psychologically engaged and enraged in barrios. In validation, the message that the institutions are willing to change will be given and received.

Discrimination produces undesirable social consequences, but the truth is that many people gain from discrimination and other social stratification mechanisms. Those who do not support it do so by their silence; an inaction is an action. Many are not aware that there is an ongoing battle of ideas over how people think about using social space and social resources. This is most evident in academia where Chicanos, for example, brought their ideas to campus in hope of sharing them. Higher education has an inherent setting that reinforces inequality. The powerful of academia resisted Chicanos and Chicanas by insisting upon Eurocentric, male-dominant classes and by structuring what it taught and how it taught. Herein lies the arduous struggle of la Chicana. She is caught in a hierarchical and highly selective field that protects its ideas feverishly. There is irony in the myth that university and college campuses have been places that foster free thinking. The truth is that the campus is characterized by human culture and human politics. Even when some Anglo scholars appear willing to confront their denial of discrimination in the United States, they still dictate the spheres, the areas of discussion and decide in which structures minimal change can take place.

THE ROLE OF GRIEF AND ATONEMENT

Changes will be slow because both the Chicano and Anglo communities have to not only recognize their losses but to also grieve for them. Each community and each individual will grieve and come to acceptance and trust at their own pace. The pace will be based upon their community history. This will not be a process where everyone is ready at the same time and work with those who want to work must progress cautiously. The difficulty in healing from historical trauma will be that those trying to fix the problem might not be those who fed the antagonism. Thus, some members of the community who believe they have real power might be resistant to attempts of apology and atonement. Also resistant will be those addicted to the struggle, those who have to learn to live in peace, those who are stuck on anger, or those in the position of being the victim. Some Chicanos will want to retaliate and hurt the Anglo population, but most Chicanos want to end the destructive situation. For many, watching their culture and their people in constant struggle is painful. Many are in a state of denial, many are already mourning. Many have dealt with mourning and will want to forget, or forgive, and move onward.

Atonement has to do with making up for past mistakes, bad deeds, or things that were done incorrectly. In community healing, these attempts can be in the form of a public announcement that says, "We the people of this community apologize for the discrimination some of our people have endured in our community"; or it can be in the form of a program sponsored by the city that makes clear that Chicano people have suffered and survived discrimination. These programs will have to be repeated frequently. For rapid results, I recommend once a month for one year, followed by six times a year for two more years. This suggestion is based on the belief that an action has to be repeated 21 to 35 times before it becomes habit. Needless to say, these programs should integrate the arts and elements of the spiritual community and must allow for dialogue before disbanding. I also very heavily suggest, as a starting mechanism, that research into the survival skills of the population be documented. Here is where the local Chicano Studies Department and its students can play a major role.

At a theoretical level this appears relatively easy. It will require, however, that dominant cultural members witness Chicano anger and be willing to make atonement. Chicano anger can be channeled into art exhibits, poetry readings, the theater, and other entities that will graphically exhibit the anger and depression, which is nothing more than internalized anger, in a socially acceptable manner. This is a necessary step in grieving for the historical trauma of a group of people. It is a necessary step in healing the loss of self-esteem, the physical and emotional beatings in school and in the media, and the community displacement from resources such as political representation and the promise of the United States to all its legal citizens.

At some point the Chicanos will have to demonstrate that they forgive past ills. This does not mean they will forget. In fact, forgetting might not be a good idea. Remembering and learning from the past builds a solid foundation, lest the mistakes be repeated. When Chicanos heal from losses, physical and emotional attacks, the death of major parts of their culture, they will heal in the physical, emotional, and spiritual realm. They can take guidance from their religious and spiritual beliefs. In these healings they can find liberation. This process can begin in kindergarten and preschool. We need to go beyond offering students skills in reading, writing, and math. We need to make them culturally literate.

REFERENCES

Fanon, Frantz. 1963. *The Wretched of the Earth*. New York: Grove Press.
Memmi, Albert. 1965. *The Colonizer and the Colonized*. Boston: Beacon Press.

Selected
Bibliography

Acuna, Rodolpho. 1972a. *Occupied America: The Struggle toward Chicano Liberation*. San Francisco: Canfield Press.

———. 1972b. *Occupied America: A History of Chicanos*. San Francisco: Harper and Row, 1981. 2d ed. of *Occupied America*.

Baca-Zinn, Maxine. 1975a. "Political Familialism: Toward Sex Role Equality in Chicano Families." *Aztlan: Chicano Journal of the Social Sciences and the Arts*, vol. 6 (Spring).

———. 1975b. "Chicanas: Power and Control in the Domestic Sphere." *De colores*, vol. 1, no. 3.

Baca-Zinn, Maxine, Lynn Cannon, Elizabeth Higgenbotham, and Bonnie Thorton Dill. 1986. "The Costs of Exclusionary Practices in Women's Studies." *Signs: Journal of Women in Culture and Society*, vol. 2, no. 21.

Barrera, Mario. 1979. *Race and Class in the Southwest*. Notre Dame: University of Notre Dame Press.

Benson, Margaret. 1969. "The Political Economy of Women's Liberation." *Monthly Review*, vol. 21, no. 4 (September).

Blauner, Robert. 1969. "Internal Colonialism and Ghetto Revolt." *Social Problems*, 16 (Spring): 393–408.

Blea, Irene I. 1977. "Street People: A Study of Boulder's Leftover Hippies." Unpublished paper, Boulder County Community Relations Office, Boulder, Colorado.

———. 1981. "An Analysis of Mexican American Homemaking." Unpublished paper presented at 1977 National Association of Chicano Studies Conference, Claremount, California.

———. 1988. *Toward a Chicano Science*. New York: Praeger.

———. 1991. *Bessemer: A Sociological Perspective of a Chicano Barrio*. New York: AMS Press.

———. 1991. *La Chicana and the Intersection of Race, Class, and Gender*. New York: Praeger.

Camarillo, Alberto. 1979. *Chicanos in a Changing Society*. Cambridge: Harvard University Press.

Cohen, R. 1979. *Culture, Disease and Stress among Latino Immigrants*. Washington, D.C.: Smithsonian Institution.

Coser, Lewis A. 1959. *The Function of Social Conflict*. Glencoe, Ill.: The Free Press.

Cotera, Martha. 1976. *Diosa Y Hembra*. Austin: Information Systems Development.

Dahrendorf, Ralf. 1959. *Class and Class Conflict in Industrial Society*. Stanford: Stanford University Press.

Davis, Allison, Burleigh B. Gardner, and Mary R. Gardner. 1941. *Deep South*. Chicago: University of Chicago Press.

De La Garza, R., and R. Brischetto. 1983. "The Mexican-American Electorate: Information Sources and Policy Orientation." Occasional Paper No. 2, San Antonio, Texas, Southwest Voter Registration Education Project and the Hispanic Population Studies Program of the Center for Mexican American Studies. Austin: University of Texas.

Dollard, John. 1937. *Caste and Class in a Southern Town*. New Haven: Yale University Press.

Drake, Sinclair, and Horace Cayton. 1945. *Black Metropolis*. New York: Harcourt, Brace and World, Inc.

Durkheim, Emile. 1915. *The Elementary Forms of the Religious Life*. New York: Macmillan and Free Press. Originally published in 1897.

———. 1964. *The Division of Labor in Society*. Translated by George Simpson. New York: Macmillan and Free Press. Originally published in 1893.

Enriquez, Evangelina, and Alfredo Mirande. 1979. *La Chicana: The Mexican American Woman*. Chicago: University of Chicago Press.

Fanon, Frantz. 1963. *The Wretched of the Earth*. New York: Grove Press.

Figueroa Torres, J. Jesus. 1975. *Dona Marina: Una India Ejemplar*, Mexico, D.F.: B. Costa-Amic Editor.

Frammolino, Ralph. 1994. *Los Angeles Times*, November 20.

Gans, Herbert J. 1951. "Park Forest: Birth of a Jewish Community." *Commentary* 58, Vol. 11.

———. 1962. *The Urban Villagers*. New York: The Free Press.

Garcia, Mario. 1981. *Desert Immigrant: The Mexicans of El Paso, 1880–1920*. New Haven: Yale University Press.

Garcia Rivas, Heriberto Garcia. 1988. *Cocina PreHispanica Mexicana*. Mexico, D.F.: Coleccion Panorama.

Glazer, Nathan. 1971a. "Blacks and Ethnic Groups: The Difference and the Political Difference It Makes." *Social Problems* (Spring).

———. 1971b. "The Issue of Cultural Pluralism in America Today." In *Pluralism beyond Frontier: Report of the San Francisco Consultation on Ethnicity*. San Francisco: American Jewish Committee.

———. 1974a. "Ethnicity and the Schools." *Commentary* 58 (September).

———. 1974b. "Why Ethnicity?" *Commentary* 58 (October).

———. 1975. *Affirmative Discrimination: Ethnic Inequality and Public Policy*. New York: Basic Books.

Glazer, Nathan, and Daniel P. Moynihan. 1963. *Beyond the Melting Pot: The Negroes, Puerto Ricans, Jews, Italians and Irish of New York City*. Cambridge: The M.I.T. Press.

Goffman, Erving. 1961. *Asylums*. Chicago: Aldine Publishing Company.

Gomez Tagle, Silvia, Adrian Garcia Valdes, and Lourdes Grobet. *National Museum of Anthropology: Mexico*. Translation by Joan Ingram-Eiser. Mexico, D.F.: Distribucion Cultural Especializada.

Grebler, L., Joan Moore, and Ralph Guzman. 1970. *The Mexican American People*. New York: Free Press.

Green, Reyna, and Frank W. Porter III. 1992. *Women in American Indian Society*. New York: Chelsea House Publishers.

Halverson, James. 1978. *Bar Room Brethren*. Pueblo, Colo.: Colorado State Hospital Printshop.

Harrington, Michael. 1963. *The Other American: Poverty in the United States*. Baltimore: Penguin.

Heller, Celia. 1966. *Mexican American Youth; Forgotten Youth at the Crossroads*. New York: Random House.

Hernandez, Deluvina. 1970. *Mexican American Challenge to a Sacred Cow*. Los Angeles: Chicano Cultural Center.

Hollingshead, August B. 1949. *Elmtown's Youth*. New York: John Wiley and Sons, Inc.

Jaquez, Rolando. 1976. "What the Tape Recorder Has Created: A Broadly Based Exploration into Contemporary Oral History Practice." *Aztlan: International Journal of Chicano Studies* (Spring).

Julip, Kay. 1994. *Vista*, vol. 9, no. 6 (February 9).

Kiev, Aria. 1968. *Curanderismo, Mexican American Folk Psychiatry*. New York: Free Press.

Kluckhohn, Florence, and Fred L. Strodbeck. 1961. *Variations in Value Orientations*. Evanston, Ill.: Raw Peterson.

Leibow, Elliot. 1967. *Tally's Corner: A Study of Negro Streetcorner Men*. Boston: Little, Brown and Company.

Lewis, Oscar. 1959. *Five Families: Mexican Case Studies in the Culture of Poverty*. New York: Basic Books.

———. 1960. *The Children of Sanchez*. New York: Random House.

———. 1965. *La Vida: A Puerto Rican Family in the Culture of Poverty—San Juan and New York*. New York: Random House.

———. 1966. "The Culture of Poverty." *Scientific American* (October).

Leyburn, James. 1968. "William Graham." In David J. Sills, ed., *International Encyclopedia of the Social Sciences*. Vol. 16. New York: Macmillan and Free Press.

Lizarraga, Sylvia. 1988. "Hacia Una Teoria Para La Liberacion de la Mujer." In Juana R. Garcia, Jualia Curry Rodriguez, and Clara Lomas, eds., *Ties of Challenge: Chicanos and Chicanas in American Society*. Texas: University of Houston Press, Mexican-American Studies Program, Monograph Series No. 6.

Lindsmith, Alfred. 1947. *Addiction and Opiates*. Chicago: Aldine Publishing Co.

Lofland, John. 1971. *Analyzing Social Settings: A Guide to Qualitative Observation and Analysis*. Belmont: Wadsworth Publishing Company.

Lynd, Robert S., and Helen M. Lynd. 1929. *Middletown: A Study of Contemporary American Culture*. New York: Harcourt, Brace.

———. 1937. *Middletown in Transition: A Study in Cultural Conflicts*. New York: Harcourt, Brace.

Mannino, F. V., and M. F. Shore. 1976. "Perceptions of Social Support by Spanish-speaking Youth with Implications for Program Development." *Journal of School Health*.

Marin, Gerardo, and Barbara VanOss Marin. 1991. *Research with Hispanic Populations*. Newbury Park: Sage Publications.

Marin, G., and H. C. Triandes. 1985. "Allocentrism as an Important Characteristic of the Behavior of Latin Americans and Hispanics." In R. Dian-Guerrero, ed., *Cross-cultural and National Studies in Social Psychology*. Amsterdam: Elsevier Science Publishers.

Marindale, Don. 1968. "Verstehen." In David J. Sills, ed., *International Encyclopedia of the Social Sciences*. Vol. 16. New York: Macmillan and Free Press.

Marx, Karl, and Friedrich Engels. 1965. "Communist Manifesto." In Arthur Mendel, ed., *Essential Works of Marxism*. New York: Bantam Books. Originally published in 1848.

Mead, Margaret. 1935. *Sex and Temperament in Three Primitive Societies*. New York: William Morrow.

Medsen, William. 1964. *Mexican Americans of South Texas*. New York: Holt, Rinehart and Winston.

Melville, Margaritta B. 1980. *Twice a Minority*. St. Louis: C. V. Mosby Press.

Memmi, Albert. 1965. *The Colonizer and the Colonized*. Boston: Beacon Press.

Moore, Joan W., Robert Garcia, Carlos Garcia, Luis Cerda, and Frank Valencia. 1979. *Homeboys: Gangs, Drugs and Prison in the Barrios of Los Angeles*. Philadelphia: Temple University Press.

Munoz, Carlos J. 1972. *The Politics of Urban Protest: A Model of Political Analysis*. Claremont, Calif.: Claremont Graduate School of Government.

Myrdal, Gunnar. 1944. *American Dilemma*. New York: Pantheon.

National Women's History Project. 1992. "Adelante Mujeres." Video. Washington, D.C.

Nisbet, Robert A. 1962. *Community and Power: A Study in the Ethics of Order and Freedom*. New York: Oxford University Press.

Orozco, Cynthia. 1986. *Chicana Voices: Intersections of Class, Race, and Gender*. Austin: CMAS Publications.

Padilla, Raymond V. 1985. *Chicano Studies at the University of California at Berkeley: En Busca del Campus y la Communidad*. Ph.D. diss., School of Education, University of California, Berkeley.

———. 1987. "Chicano Studies Revisited: Still in Search of the Campus and the Community." In Alfredo Gonzalez and David Sandoval, comps., *A Symposium of Chicano Studies: Proceedings of the National Association for Chicano Studies Southern California FOCO*. Los Angeles: California State University.

Poplin, Dennis E. 1972. *Communities: A Survey of Theories and Methods of Research*. New York: Macmillan Publishing Co., Inc.

Quiroz, Joaquin. 1994. *Vista*, Vol. 9, No. 6 (February 9).

Roco, Raymond A. 1976. "The Chicano in Social Sciences: Traditional Concepts, Myths, and Images." *Aztlan: International Journal of Chicano Studies* (Spring). Los Angeles: Chicano Cultural Center.

Roiz, Carmen Teresa. 1994. *Vista*, Vol. 9, No. 6 (February 9).

Romano, Octavio. 1968. "The Anthropology and Sociology of the Mexican Americans: The Distortion of Mexican-American History." *El Grito* (Fall).

Samora, Julian, and Richard A. Lamanna. 1967. *Mexican Americans in a Midwest Metropolis: A Study of East Chicago*. Los Angeles: Mexican American Project.

Saunders, Lyle. 1954. *Cultural Differences and Medical Care of the Spanish Speaking People in the Southwest*. New York: Russell Sage Foundation.

Scamehorn, H. Lee. 1966. *Pioneer Steelmakers in the West*. Boulder, Colo.: Pruett Publishing Company.

Schulz, David A. 1969. *Coming Up African American: Patterns of Ghetto Socialization*. Englewood Cliff, N.J.: Prentice-Hall, Inc.

Suttles, Gerald D. 1982. *The Structure of Sociological Theory*, 3d ed. Hornewood, Ill.: Dorsey Press.

Thomas, W. I., and Dorothy Thomas. 1928. *The Child in America: Behavior Problems and Programs*. New York: Alfred A. Knopf.

Trotter, Robert, and Juan Antonio Chevira. 1981. *Curanderismo: Mexican American Health and Religion*. Athens: University of Georgia Press.

Trujillo, Marcella. 1975. "The Road to Canon: The Road to La Pinta." In *An Anthology of Chicano Literature*. Austin: Chicano Studies Center.

Tuck, Ruth. 1946. *Not with the Fist: Mexican Americans in a Southwest City*. New York: Harcourt, Brace.

Turner, J. H. 1972. *Patterns of Social Organization*. New York: McGraw-Hill.

United States Bureau of Census, 1985. "Persons of Spanish Origin in the United States." Current Population Reports, Series 20, No. 310 (July), No. 328 (August). Washington D.C.: U.S. Government Printing Office, March.

———. 1993. "We the American Hispanics," (November).

Valle, R., and C. Martinez. 1980. "Natural Networks among Mexicano Elderly in the United States: Implications for Mental Health." In M. R. Miranda and R. A. Ruiz, eds., *Chicano Aging and Mental Health*. Washington, D.C.: Government Printing Office.

Veyna, Angelina F. 1986. "Women in Early New Mexico: A Preliminary View." In T. Cordova et al., eds., *Chicana Voices: Intersections of Class, Race and Gender*. Austin: CMAS Publications, University of Texas Press.

Vidich, Arthur J., and Joseph Bensman. 1953. *Small Town in Mass Society*. Princeton, N.J.: Princetown University Press.

Volkart, E. H. "W. I. Thomas." 1968. In David J. Sills, ed., *International Encyclopedia of the Social Sciences*. Vol. 16. New York: Macmillan and Free Press.

Warner, W. Lloyd. 1941. *Yankee City*. New Haven: Yale University Press.

Warner, W. Lloyd, and Paul S. Lunt. 1941. *The Social Life of a Modern Community*. New Haven: Yale University Press.

———. 1942. *The Status System of a Modern Community*. New Haven: Yale University Press.

Warner, W. Lloyd, et al. 1949. *Democracy in Jonesville*. New York: Harper and Row.

Weber, Max. 1958. *The Protestant Ethic and the Spirit of Capitalism*. New York: Charles Scribner's Sons.

———. "Religion." 1970a. In H. H. Gerth and C. Wright Mills, trans. *From Max Weber: Essays in Sociology*. New York: Oxford University Press. Originally published in 1920.

———. 1970b. "Science as a Vocation." In H. H. Gerth and C. Wright Mills, trans. *From Max Weber: Essays in Sociology*. New York: Oxford University Press. Originally published in 1918.

West, James. 1945. *Plainville, U.S.A.* New York: Columbia University Press.

Wirth, Louis, 1928. *The Ghetto*. Chicago: University of Chicago Press.

Whyte, William Foote. 1955. *Street Corner Society*. Chicago: University of Chicago Press.

Ybarra, Leonarda. 1977. "Conjugal Role Relationships in the Chicano Family," Ph.D. diss., University of California, Berkeley.

———. 1982a. "Marital Decision-Making and the Role of Machismo in the Chicano Family." *De colores*, vol. 6, nos. 1 and 2.

———. 1982b. "When Wives Work: The Impact on the Chicano Family." *Journal of Marriage and the Family*, vol. 44 (February).

Index

About the Author

IRENE ISABEL BLEA is the chairperson of the Department of Chicano Studies at California State University in Los Angeles. Blea received her Ph.D. from the University of Colorado and has been affiliated with the University of New Mexico, University of Texas at Austin, and Metropolitan State College of Denver. Her previous books include *La Chicana and the Intersection of Race, Class and Gender* (Praeger, 1991), *Bessemer: A Sociological Perspective of a Chicano Barrio* (1991), and *Toward A Chicano Social Science* (Praeger, 1988).

ISBN 0-275-94974-5

90000>

HARDCOVER BAR CODE